Waris Dirie is an internationally renowned model and was a face of Revlon skin-care products. In 1997 she was appointed by the United Nations as special ambassador for women's rights in Africa, in its effort to eliminate the practice of female genital mutilation. Waris Dirie lives in Austria.

Jeanne D'Haem, Ph.D. is the author of *The Last Camel*, a collection of stories about Northern Somalia or Somaliland as it is known now. She lived in a Somali village as a Peace Corps teacher in the late 60s. Her work has been published by Scribners, The New Rivers Press and the *New York Times*. She lectures and speaks at book clubs throughout the United States.

Also by Waris Dirie

Desert Flower
Desert Children
Saving Safa

desert dawn

waris dirie

and jeanne d'haem

virago

VIRAGO

First published by Virago Press in 2002
This edition published by Virago Press in 2004

11 13 15 14 12 10

Copyright © Waris Dirie 2002

A CIP catalogue record for this book
is available from the British Library.

ISBN 978-1-84408-008-3

Typeset in Baskerville by M Rules
Printed and bound in Great Britain by
Clays Ltd, St Ives plc

Papers used by Virago are from well-managed forests
and other responsible sources.

MIX
Paper from
responsible sources
FSC® C104740

Virago Press
An imprint of
Little, Brown Book Group
Carmelite House
50 Victoria Embankment
London EC4Y 0DZ

An Hachette UK Company
www.hachette.co.uk

www.virago.co.uk

To You

To sit and dream, to sit and read,
To sit and learn about the world
Outside our world of here and now—
    Our problem world—
To dream of vast horizons of the soul
Through dreams made whole,
Unfettered, free—help me!
    All you who are dreamers too,
    Help me to make
    Our world anew.
I reach out my dreams to you.

Langston Hughes

Africa You are Beautiful

Has anyone told you
    you are beautiful
Africa?
    Your full body
and sensuous lips
    have kissed my soul
and Africa, I am bound to you
    by the drumbeat of
my heart that pumps the
    blood of my birthright
and you are mine.

Rashidah Ismaili

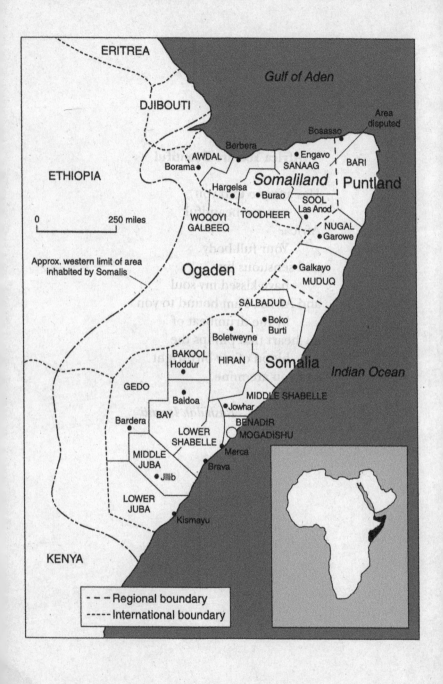

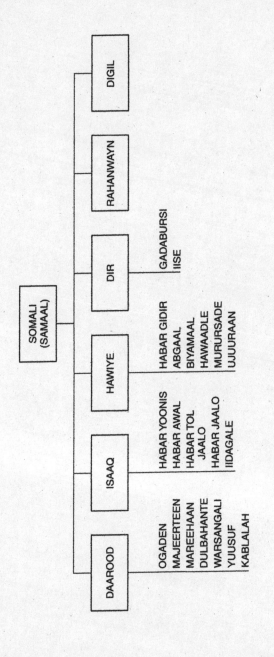

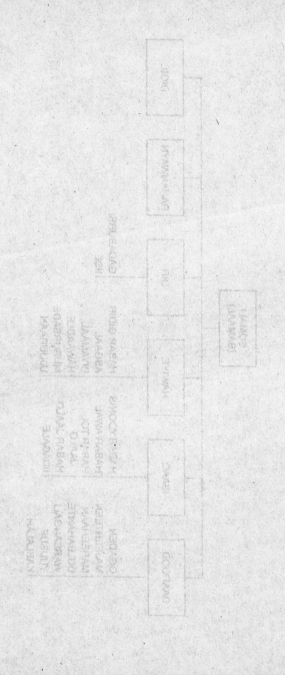

1
desert dreaming

A man came to God's Messenger and said, 'O Messenger of God, who is the most entitled to the best of my friendship?' The Prophet said, 'Your mother.' The man said, 'Then who?' The Prophet said, 'Your mother.' The man further said, 'Then who?' The Prophet said, 'Your mother.' The man said again, 'Then who?' The Prophet said, 'Then your father.'

Somali Traditional Saying about the Prophet Mohammed

In Somalia the devils are white. They are called *djinn* and they are everywhere. Everywhere! They crawl inside people and animals and make them sick. They play tricks and make you crazy. When you put something down and then suddenly it's gone when you turn around, you know that a *djinn* is sitting on it. My mother shouted at them, 'Hey! Devil! Get away from my things! They are not for you; you are not wanted around here.' My mother knew all about the *djinn* and how to get rid of them. She knew the special chants and exactly what tree leaves or bark would get the *djinn* out when we were sick. She cooked flowers and roots or gave them to us raw to chew on and kept special leaves and fungus in a leather pouch. She could read smoke, the wind and the stars and knew when the time was right. She was well-respected because she was gifted with many magic powers. I remember when I was a little girl people brought sick animals to her.

I was born in the Somalian desert. I don't know how many children my mother had. Many were babies born to be buried. Like most Somalis, we cared for camels and goats and lived on their milk. Following tradition, my brothers usually took care of the camels, and the girls watched over the smaller animals.

My family never stayed in one place for more than three or four weeks. After the animals ate the grass we had to move and find something else for them to eat.

One day when I had lived for about eight *gu* or rainy seasons, I was looking after our goats not too far from where my family was camped. That morning I scrambled down and back up the steep sandy banks of the *tuug* or dry river bed to a place I had seen the day before. It had some fresh grasses and a few acacia trees. The bigger goats would stand up on their hind legs and pull branches down so they could eat the bottom leaves. In the rainy season goats stay around the settlement without much care, but in the dry season you have to search for the grassy spots and you can't take your eyes off the animals for a split second because predators are lurking behind every bush. I sat in the shade during the hot afternoon singing little songs to myself, and playing with the dolls that I had made out of sticks. I always knew what I wanted to be. Even as a little child I had a vision. I knew the man I was going to marry. I played that I had a house. I used little rocks for my goats and bigger rocks for my camels and cattle. I built a big round house with sand. Wet sand was the best because I could make it exactly like our own little hut, only mine was better because I could make it just the style I wanted. My mother built our house and covered it with mats she wove from long grasses so it could be quickly loaded on our camels when we moved. My play house was safe and nice like hers. I had a husband and children and we lived far away from my family.

The sun's heat seemed to keep everything in place in the middle of the day. I could see up and down the sandy *tuug* for a long way in both directions. In the evening, on my way back to our camp, I had seen the wicked yellow eyes of a pack of hyenas watching me and the goats. I was scared because hyenas are clever and if you aren't on your guard they will get between you and one of the goats. You have to make yourself big and fearless so that they won't sense that you are afraid.

Whitey, my mother's favorite goat, looked up and sniffed the air so I looked too. I saw a man walking along the edge of the *tuug* pulling a camel after him with a braided rope. Usually camels follow along behind a lead camel who wears a wooden camel bell. It makes a hollow sound and the others follow single file like elephants holding on to each other's tail with their trunks. This funny camel was twisting and turning to one side in a strange way. It was not fighting, it was shaking and frothing at the mouth. Every now and then it would stop entirely and tremble. That animal had a *djinn*, there was a devil in it for sure. I watched the man yank the poor thing along the ridge of the hill. Suddenly, it fell over, all scrambled up in a heap. He shouted and yelled at it to get up. He started hitting it with a stick right on its belly but that camel just lay there twitching like crazy in the sand. I thought it must be a *hahl* or female and that she was pregnant, a valuable animal. The man sat down and put his head in his hands. I was surprised to see a grown man sit in the dirt. Nomads will stand and rest with one foot braced up against the other thigh and their arms draped over a stick across their shoulders, or sometimes we squat on the ground. I had never seen anyone beat a camel like that. In my family, camels were valuable. A man who owns camels is one with power. He can sell or trade them for a wife and buy anything else he wants. They are magic animals. My father and uncles were firm with our herd but they never beat them unless they were obstinate and would not obey them. Camels are mean and I knew to stay away from kicking feet and biting teeth.

I didn't let him see me watching, I was afraid he would hit me too. I wanted to run home and tell my mother but I didn't dare leave the goats. My father would be furious and whip me if the animals wandered off or a hyena got one of them. I stood as still as a baby gazelle surprised in the bush and hardly dared to breathe.

Finally the *hahl* stopped shaking. She looked around for a moment and seemed to realize she was lying on the ground. She jerked to put her legs underneath her belly then got up all of a sudden. Although she was graceful, like most camels, drool and foam were dripping from her mouth. The stranger got up then too – almost as though he had been through this many times – and started pulling at her again. They went down into the *tuug* and up the other side towards our camp. I thought he must be worried about this sick camel. If she died he would lose both the camel and baby and the opportunity for more.

It had been dry and hot for longer than I could remember. I knew my parents were worried even though they didn't say anything. We didn't have much water because the wells in the *tuug* were dryer and dryer. We had moved our camp several times to find water for the animals. A newly born camel had died during the night. My younger brother, who we called Old Man because he was born with white hair, found her in the morning. Old Man always seemed to know things before anyone else did even though he was so young. My father poked the tiny thing. It was all legs and neck. Father stared at the cloudless sky. When it was dry he constantly looked to the sky and Allah for rain. We couldn't eat the meat from the calf because in our Muslim religion it is unclean to eat an animal that has not been properly slaughtered with a knife to the throat. Vultures were already circling above us so boldly that their long wings cast a shadow every time they passed overhead. I remember the sound of the dry wind and the low murmur of my mother praying.

My mother would never miss any of her daily prayers no matter how desperate the situation. If a person is sick they only have to pray three times a day instead of five and they don't have to prostrate themselves, but my mother always prayed five times. Before Muslims pray they wash so they are clean and pure when they talk to God. *Allah, let this washing cleanse my soul* . . . We barely had enough water to stay alive or give the animals, so there was no water to wash. When Mama couldn't find water she washed herself with sand. Five times a day, she carefully dug some earth out from under a bush so that no people or animals had walked on it. She put it between her hands and washed herself just like it was water. She rubbed it on her face and her feet. Then she would roll out her woven prayer mat and face the East, towards the holy city of Mecca, and pray, bowing and kneeling and chanting. *There is no God but God and Mohammed is His prophet* . . . The sun was our only clock. We kept time with the five daily prayers, at dawn, noon, before sunset, after sunset and night.

When my mother finished her song to Allah she rolled up her mat and put it inside our round house. She built it herself out of the long roots of the *galol* tree. She dug the flexible roots out of the ground and arched them into a dome. These were then covered with the mats she wove out of grasses. My mother was the worker in our family. She cooked the food, nursed the babies, built the house, wove the mats we slept on and made baskets and wooden spoons. She was the cook, the builder, the doctor, and my only teacher. My mother didn't say anything about the dead baby camel, she just got on with the day. 'God willing the goats will have milk this morning,' she said. She said that every day when we went to milk the goats and the camels. My mother had a way with animals. They stood quietly when she touched them. I had to put the animal's head between my legs into the folds of my dress and bend over its back to keep it from kicking or shitting in the bowl when I tried to milk them. But with Mama they seemed to want to stand next to her, to let her touch their silky teats. Mama would joke and sing while she milked.

Whitey had the most milk that morning and mother divided it for the eight of us. She looked at my father right in the eyes, something she rarely did, and when she put her bowl of milk in his hands they held it together for a moment. My papa was so strong he could pick up the biggest goat we had. He was Daarood, the biggest and toughest clan in all of Somalia. The nickname for Daarood is *Libah*, or Lion. He was taller than any man I knew and had eyes so sharp he could tell a male gazelle from a female across the plain. I knew he was handsome because I saw how women joked with him to get his attention.

I watched the stranger lead the camel into our camp. I knew I couldn't leave the goats but I really wanted to know what was happening with the bitter man and his strange camel. Suddenly I saw Old Man walking along the other side of the *tuug* looking for wood. '*Calli, calli*, come here, come here,' I called, cupping my hand towards him. I wondered why he was looking for firewood. He bounded down and stood at the bottom of the *tuug*.

'What's going on?' I called to him.

'Mama wants a bigger fire,' he said. 'A cousin brought a sick camel to see if she can heal it.' Old Man had a sweet face under his startling white hair, and round golden brown eyes, the color of frankincense. He looked like my mother who was the real beauty in our family. No one would say so though because as soon as you did it would attract a *djinn* and something bad was bound to happen to him.

'Old Man,' I called, 'come over here and I'll let you watch the goats. I need to see Mama.' My brother hesitated, but he was eager to be considered old enough to look after goats. Boys work their way up to herding camels, the most prestigious job, by looking after sheep and goats when they are small. Usually I wouldn't let him near them saying he would scare them. Today I wanted to see what was happening enough to risk a beating if Old Man did lose one of the goats.

I worried that someone would notice that I left my duty and so I crept cautiously towards our house. However, nobody took any notice of another skinny little kid. I could smell smoke from the fire and tea. I saw my older sister pour the tea into one of our two glasses. She held the pot up high and poured it in a long thin stream to release the spicy smell into the air. She served it to my father and the stranger. She never looked directly in their faces, only at the ground, like a proper woman. I wondered why Mama wasn't serving the tea to the men.

The camel by the side of our hut began jerking and twitching again. The camel was having a fit! My mother crouched nearby in the long afternoon shadow of our hut and watched. She followed everything that animal did, studying it as if she was going to buy it. The camel was light brown, almost the color of a lion's mane, and her belly was swollen with a baby. Her flesh was torn and her knees were bloody from falling down. Mama looked so hard at this animal it seemed like she was transfixed – but not with fear. I squatted silently behind my mother, I wanted to be a healer and I wanted to find out what she did.

My mother looked over at the men drinking tea. The man was a distant cousin of my father. He was not as tall as Papa and he had an odd-shaped head and a long neck like an ostrich. She watched him drink his tea and talk with my father about some political party, and fighting in the Ogaden. She was seeing what kind of a person he was. Mother looked at the camel's dried blood and hairs on the end of his stick. She got up and slowly approached the camel, cooing softly '*Allah Bah Wain*'; 'God is Great,' she chanted. She put her outstretched hand on the camel's cheek then slowly, delicately, drew her fingertips down the long neck, over the top of the shoulder to the belly. The camel didn't move away but kept shaking the whole time. Mama ran her hand all over the big stomach feeling the new life within. The animal was so thin that her ribs stood out even though she was carrying a baby. Mama put her ear on the beast's belly and listened for the heartbeat of a new life. She slowly backed away and then wiped her hand through some of the froth dripping out of the animal's black lips. She rubbed it back and forth in her fingers and tasted it. She opened the camel's mouth and looked at the teeth and the thick tongue. When the animal peed she picked up some of the wet sand and smelled it. She seemed to be waiting for the right time and watched the sun slowly sink behind the distant hills. She knew how the stars moved and when the seasons would change from the *gu* rains to the *hagaa* or dry season. She knew just when things needed to be done and when it was better to wait.

Mama took the braided halter and tugged on it backwards. She coaxed the camel to *faardisimo* or sit. I saw its long ears turn one after the other in the direction of my mother's voice. The beast sat down heavily. First it knelt on its front knees, then the back legs folded up and she sat down with her legs tucked under her. Camels are trained to kneel because they are too tall to load standing up. Mama squatted down so that the camel's head was at exactly the same height as her face.

Everything in the camp got very quiet. The men stopped talking, women stopped banging the cooking pots. Even the smoke from the fire seemed to be waiting. Mama reached up and placed her hands on either side of the animal's face as if it were a human child. She looked at it right in the eyes – then she slapped the camel with gentle slaps. 'Get out you devil, get out of here! You are not wanted.' She knew exactly how many times to slap and just how hard to get the *djinn* to move on. She took the leather amulet she wore around her neck and with holy words from the Koran touched it to the animal's nose, the entrance to the soul. The animal kept absolutely still for several breaths. Then the trembling stopped and it started chewing like camels do when they are resting.

Mama got up and covered her face with her headscarf before she went to my father and his cousin. She looked at the ground and told them that a bad spirit, a certain *djinn*, had got into the camel and caused it to have fits. 'She will deliver her baby soon,' Mama told them, 'before the moon is dark. The shaking *djinn* has gone now, but the camel needs to rest and to have extra food and water until she delivers her child. That will help her to fight off the *djinn* if it comes back.'

'She won't eat,' the cousin said.

'She is frightened of the devil,' my mother explained. 'You must pet her and talk calmly to her, then she will eat and get fat.'

'*Hiiyea*, I see,' my father and his cousin nodded at the same time.

'We shall slaughter a goat, make a feast, and say many prayers to Allah to keep away this *djinn*,' Father said. I must have jumped when he said goat because he looked over and saw me. He reached out and grabbed my arm before I could run away. He drew me over to him and slapped me so hard that I could taste the blood running out of my nose. Before he could hit me again I wriggled free and raced back to the grazing area. The bottom of the *tuug* was darker than the sky and I couldn't see in the growing darkness. I tripped over jagged rocks and the thorns on the *galol* bushes tore at my skin. In the darkness I heard Baby, one of the goats, bleating. We called him Baby because he always made so much noise. Old Man was walking in the *tuug* with the goats obediently following along behind him. I was so glad to see his silver hair in the shadows I cried and couldn't stop. It felt like my arm was broken and I knew my father would beat me again when we returned. I wanted my mother's hands on my face instead of that vicious slap. Why was a camel more important than a daughter?

Several years later, when I was considered old enough to be married off, I ran away from my father and the harsh Somali life, but in many ways the Western world was harsher. A father's slap was better than the loneliness I found in the modern world. When I found myself alone in a hotel, in America or Britain, with devils spinning the room all around, I longed for a human touch – even a slap – from hands that loved me. My eyes would be burning and swollen from crying. I felt that I was lost and that my life had no direction. In Somalia, family is everything; relationships are as essential as water and milk. The worst insult you could hurl was 'May gazelles play in your house.' It means: may your family disappear. Gazelles are shy and would never come near a house unless it was abandoned. For us, to be alone is worse than death. I had no family nearby and my relationship with my fiancé, Dana, had deteriorated. I wanted to find my mother, but when I asked a Somali man about Somalia, he said, 'Forget about Somalia. It does not exist any more.' His eyes were flat, as if the light had gone out of his heart. It was as if he said I didn't have a mother. It can't be true. If there is no Somalia, then what am I? My language, culture and customs are unique, even the way we look is particular to us. How could a country disappear like water in a *tuug*?

Now it was 2000, nineteen years after I had run away. My country was torn apart by famine and war and I didn't know what had happened to my family. I was in Los Angeles to give a talk about female genital mutilation. I agreed to speak even though it was difficult for me. In 1995 I had broken a strong traditional taboo and talked publicly about my own circumcision. I had become a United Nations spokeswoman on the subject, but every time I spoke it brought back painful emotional and physical memories. As a child I actually begged my mother to have it done because I heard it would make me clean and pure. When I was only as tall as a goat, my mother held me while an old woman cut off my clitoris and the inner parts of my vagina and sewed the wound closed. She left only a tiny matchstick-sized opening for urine and menstrual blood. At the time I had no idea what was going on because we never, ever talked about it. The topic is taboo. My beautiful sister Halimo died from it. Although no one in my family would tell me, I am certain she bled to death or died from an infection. The *midgaan* women who do the circumcision use a razor blade or a knife sharpened on a stone for the cutting. They are considered untouchables in Somali society because they come from a tribe that is not descended from the Prophet Mohammed. They use a paste of myrrh to stop the blood but when things go wrong we don't have penicillin. Later, when a girl is married, the groom tries to force open the bride's infibulation on the wedding night. If the opening is too small, the girl is opened with a knife. After years of struggle I realized that this is actually mutilation but I still felt anxious when I spoke out about it – I was afraid something bad would happen to me for breaking the code of silence.

It was late when I got to the hotel where the conference was being held and I didn't know there were events going on in many different rooms. I had trouble figuring out where I was supposed to be. Finally someone directed me to the ballroom. When I opened the double doors I was stunned to see five or six hundred people in the giant room. The chair, Nancy Leno, was already sitting on the stage with the other panelists. In situations like this, I have learned to act as if I know exactly what I am doing. Taking a deep breath, I held my head high and walked up the little stairs on the side of the stage. Nancy got up and came over to greet me. She was reassuring and her graciousness calmed me down.

I spoke on a panel with an attorney who specialized in securing asylum and a Sudanese doctor. Both women had facts and numbers to back up everything they said. It is estimated that some 70 million women have been victims of the ancient tradition, though the roots of the procedure are lost in its great secrecy. Different levels of severity are practiced around the world. *Sunna* is the removal of the clitoris. Excision removes the labia as well. Girls in Somalia suffer the most severe form of female genital mutilation called Pharonic circumcision or infibulation. The clitoris and the inner lips of the vagina are cut off and the wound is sewn shut leaving only a small opening for blood and urine. The doctor said that female genital mutilation (FGM) was performed on 84 percent of Egyptian girls between three and thirteen. It is no longer limited to Muslim countries either – over 6,000 young girls in Western countries now suffer this procedure.

I tried to explain what had happened to me as a little girl in Somalia and my difficulties with urination and menstruation. My mother told me not to drink so the opening would remain small and to sleep on my back so the wound would heal flat and clean. She believed this would ensure my future because girls with intact genitals are considered unclean and sexually driven sluts. No mother would consider such a girl a proper wife for her son. My mother believed, like all my people, that infibulation was ordered in the Koran. Talking about my genital mutilation was both a blessing and a curse. I was glad people wanted to do something about this cruel custom, but over and over I had to relive all the pain and misery it caused in my life. Every time I spoke out about female genital mutilation I spoke against something my mother, my father and my people believe. I denounced my family and a tradition that was very important to them. I wanted to heal women who had been through this painful experience but it made me an enemy in my own country. If I still lived with my family I would never have dared to say anything in public. It made me frightened and anxious every time I spoke about female genital mutilation. There are things you don't talk about in my culture; we do not speak about the dead or say that someone is beautiful. We have many secrets because if you talk about it openly, you are sure that something terrible will happen. It upset me when the attorney said that female circumcision was actually torture. My mother did not have me tortured. She thought she was making me a pure woman. One who would be a good wife and mother to her children and an honor to her family.

After I spoke, many people in the audience wanted to know more, but I was ashamed and I felt like I couldn't say anything else. I felt my part of the presentation had been terrible. I left the auditorium by the side door, got on the elevator and pushed the button for the nineteenth floor. It always scares me to go up so high in buildings. As a child my world was flat and open, and feeling my body go straight up in a little box always makes me anxious, it is so unnatural.

My hand shook as I pushed the cardboard key thing in the slit and I put the 'do not disturb' sign on the door. I closed the brown drapes to keep out the sunshine. It was a clear cloudless day and it reminded me of my home in the south of Somalia. I looked in the minibar and a *djinn* smiled at me. It said, 'Welcome! Welcome!' I gathered up the little bottles of gin and rum and scotch and crawled into the bed with them. Every bottle was a different devil and I drank them all – one after the other.

My mother could have kept the devils away but I had no

idea where she was or if she would even know me any more. She didn't understand photographs let alone modeling. Our clan would tear my eyes out if they knew what I was saying about our culture. I wanted to be a healer like my mother, but speaking out against FGM insulted her. She taught me never to say anything mean because you send it out to the universe, it's out there and you can never get it back. A black angel, Malick, sits on one shoulder, and a white devil, Behir, sits on the other. When Behir made my mother say something unkind she would ask Malick to take it back. 'Take it back, take it back,' she would say right away, before it got too far. 'I take it back, I take it back,' I cried, but I knew it was too late. All of the terrible things I said about my people were all over the universe. There was no taking it back.

I wanted to stay in that room forever. I put the sheets over my head and burrowed down like a tortoise. I was frightened and alone – a worthless failure. Big sobs started in my chest and pushed themselves right out of my mouth; they had been stuffed down my throat for a long time. Fear punctured every thought. When I finally fell asleep I dreamed that I couldn't find the goats, they had wandered off and I looked everywhere. My feet were bleeding from stumbling over the rocks and thorn bushes. I could hear them bleating, but I couldn't find them. When I woke up I found that I was the one crying.

Even though I really didn't care what happened to me, suicide was unthinkable. My mother told me she knew a girl of fifteen who burned herself to death because her parents refused to allow her to marry the boy she loved. They did not bury her and even the vultures would not approach the body. When I turned on the water in the gleaming tiled bathroom to take a shower, all I could think about was my mother washing herself with dirt and here I let gallons of water flow down the drain. I stared at myself in the wall of mirrors. My mother is an extraordinarily beautiful woman but she has never seen her reflection. She has no idea what her face looks like. I looked at my body and felt ashamed of my legs. They are bowed due to childhood malnutrition and I have been fired from modeling jobs because of them. Like the devils who wait at crossroads, the threat of starvation is always there in Somalia. I wondered if anyone in my family was still alive. News was rare and always terrible. My brother, Old Man, was dead, and my sisters Aman and Halimo were too. Stray bullets that came through the kitchen window in Mogadishu, during the political struggles between tribes, had killed my mother's funny brother, Uncle Wold'ab, who looked just like her. My mother had been shot but she lived. I didn't know about anyone else.

I had run away when I was about thirteen years old because my father tried to marry me off to an old man. In Somalia men must pay a bride price for a virgin and this balding old man leaned on a walking stick and offered several camels for me. A woman doesn't have much choice in the matter; women have to get married. There is no other way to live in the desert; there are no jobs for single women other than prostitution or begging. Somehow, I knew that herding goats and waiting on an old man was not for me. I defied my father and ran away. My mother helped me; I don't really know why. Perhaps she didn't want me to have a bad husband. She taught me the song:

> *It is you who travels into the dark night*
> *Only to marry an ill-chosen husband*
> *Who beats you with a shepherd's crook*
> *In the scuffle it is your headscarf that comes undone.*

Now, alone and drunk with devils all around me, I longed for Mama. I knew that she could help me. After I had my son Aleeke, I ached for my own mother, for her arms around me and her voice low in my ear whispering, 'It's going to be all right.' No matter how much has passed between you, no matter how different your life's journey – you want your mother when you have a child. Every time I held my little Aleeke, now three years old, I missed my home in Africa, and my mother who is part of Africa.

My mother believes in Allah with every drop of blood in her body. She can't breathe or do anything without Allah. She can't pound the grain or milk the goats without saying thank you to God. That's how I was taught to live and that's what I love about her. Living in the West I'd lost the kind of life where you are in touch with God at every step. I began to feel I'd lose everything if I didn't go back to my soul's home in the desert.

My name, Waris, means Desert Flower in Somali. The oval petals of the desert flower are sort of yellowish-orange and this little bush bends low to hold Allah's earth between her roots. In Somalia sometimes it can be a year between the blessing of rains and yet somehow this plant stays alive. When the rains finally do come you will see flowers blooming the very next day. They appear out of the cracks in the earth as if they were nomadic butterflies. These delicate little blossoms decorate the desert when nothing else survives. Once I asked my mother, 'How did you find that name for me?'

My mother just made a kind of joke about it, she said, 'I guess because you are special.'

The thing that comes to my mind about my name is that I am a survivor, like the desert flower. My soul says it too. After all I have been through I feel like I'm 130 years old – sometimes more. I know I have been here before over and over. When I considered all the good and bad things in my life, I knew without a doubt that somehow I would manage to survive. I don't know why my mother chose that plant, I don't know why Allah chose me – but the two go together perfectly. I know that.

If you are raised in Somalia, then you know what it is to get up and walk when you have no strength. That's what I did, I got out of that bed and I moved on. I knew that I wanted to find my mother. I wanted to return to the place where I was born and see it with new eyes. I just didn't know how to do it, it seemed impossible to find my family – almost as impossible as a camel girl becoming a fashion model.

2

alone

A woman without relatives dances with her children on her back

Somali proverb

Back in New York, the travel agent looked at me like I was crazy. My friends said, 'Have you seen the newspapers? Mogadishu is a war zone.' Dana flatly refused to even talk about going to Somalia. He wanted his band to be famous and worked all the time on his music. I desperately wanted to see if I could find my family again, but no one in New York City was helpful or supportive of the idea. 'You better call the state department and see if it's safe,' the agent said. 'Did you know that Somalia is one of the world's most dangerous places?' When I got the information about Somalia I found terrible warnings: the United States warns against all travel in Somalia. Somalia has no functioning government. The present political situation is one of anarchy, marked by inter-clan fighting and random banditry. Kidnapping, rape and murder are frequently reported. There is no national government to offer assistance, nor any police protection. The northern region, the self-declared Republic of Somaliland, which formed in 1991, is less dangerous but there is no diplomatic presence in the country.

The airline agent didn't know if there were flight connections into Somalia. 'I have no idea how you could even make such a trip,' he said. 'We don't handle that sort of thing – I can't find a scheduled flight.' He also explained that in order to travel to Africa I would need to be vaccinated for yellow fever, smallpox, typhoid, hepatitis B and polio. He read from his computer screen, 'Recently there have been cases of smallpox in Somalia. You will need to take malaria pills.' It was so discouraging that I didn't even show him my passport. My British travel documents specifically forbid travel into Somalia. When I got the papers in London they did not want to be responsible for a British citizen in Somalia. 'How about a nice island in the Caribbean?' he suggested. 'Get away for a while and relax.' I didn't want to get away – I wanted to find my family.

I called people I know at the United Nations. They advised me that it was much too dangerous for me to travel in Somalia. They said I would need an armed escort everywhere I went and advised me to hire guards and a truck for the entire trip. They were concerned that fundamentalist Muslim groups might target me for an attack or kidnapping due to my public opposition to FGM.

Discouraged, I went back to my apartment. As usual, it was messy and dirty. The sink was full of dishes and take-out containers and most of a large pizza was just left on the kitchen table. I hated to see food wasted like that. When I was a child we didn't have enough to eat every day. Once my brother finished his drop of camel milk and reached over to take some of mine. I shoved his arm away and he punched me in the chest so hard I fell over and dropped the cup. That delicious milk spilled on the dirt and was gone. You couldn't lick it back out of the ground. The only thing left to drink was tears.

The kitchen faucet had not been turned off hard enough so water was dripping down the drain. I will never understand letting water run like that. In my childhood water was so precious we never wasted a drop. I still can't let the water run when I brush my teeth or wash dishes. It's a matter of respect for me; respect for the blessing of water. Nobody had opened a window; no incense was burning to add a little freshness to the air. Frankincense and myrrh come from Somalia and we always burn it to welcome a guest, for a bride or a new baby. When her husband comes back from a journey a woman will stand over the little burner and fill her skirts and her hair with the scent.

Dana was out and Aleeke was with his grandmother. I picked up the mail and bills from the floor to see what needed to be paid so things would not be shut off. That apartment was full of *djinn* and troubles. When Dana finally did come back we had one gigantic and all-out row. It ended with me shouting 'Get out, you are not wanted here!' Then I went to see my friends and had some beer to calm down. Alcohol is strictly forbidden to Muslims and my mother has never touched it. I felt guilty about drinking but first my family in Somalia was lost, now it seemed my family in the West was lost as well.

In Somalia everyone tries to keep a couple together for the good of the clans who are involved. Women do not have the same rights as men to divorce. Men decide when a marriage is over and the woman can lose her children and be left to beg without any other way to support herself. A man

can say 'I divorce you' to his wife, her family and his family. If
the families cannot get him to reconsider, then the marriage
is over. A woman is allowed to leave if he doesn't provide for
her but where will she go? What can she do? Men are
required to give a bride a number of goats or sheep as her
own. This is all she can take with her when they separate.

'Waris, good for you,' my girlfriends said, 'you have to
stand up to men or they will take advantage of you.' I was
surprised, I expected them to say, that's how men are, and
watch out he will beat you when you go back. My friend
Sharla said, 'Hey, come and stay with me for a few days.' She
had watched Dana and I argue before, and thought that
this would blow over, but I didn't think so. It had gone too
far. The truth was I wasn't feeling this relationship any more.
It was like an empty ostrich egg or a dry river bed; the life
had gone out of it. There was a song the women used to sing
and I remembered parts of it.

> *Goats need to be tended with tenderness*
> *Camels need to be tied to their tethers*
> *Your children have many needs*
> *A husband needs you to run errands for him*
> *And needs to beat you for uncommitted wrongs*

When I returned Dana wasn't home. There would be no
apologies and no making up. Aleeke was still with his
grandmother and I felt alone with the *djinn*. They were waiting and jumped in my head to keep me tossing all night. I
spent a sleepless night angry and anxious about everything
again. I knew that this was really it for us.

When Dana came home I asked him to move out. He
looked at me and shook his head. 'No, I'm not going
anywhere. If anybody is leaving it is you.' Dana said it with

such determination I knew he meant it. I stood in the doorway and watched him for a long time while he pretended that I wasn't even there. He was really saying: I'm going to make you suffer, Waris. If I have to move out, I am going to make you move too.

Moving was something that I hated to do even though I once lived a nomadic life. We all hated moving. When the goats and camels had eaten the grasses and we needed to relocate our camp, my father's tactic was to move in the middle of the night so we could get to the water and new grass before other people had touched it. We would all be sound asleep and he would start shaking us and telling us to get up and pack so we could load the camels. It was pitch black and everyone would stumble around in the dark trying to find things except my father. Somehow he could see in the dark.

'Get the cooking pot, Waris.'

'I can't find it.'

'On the other side of the fire pit.' I scurried to find it by feeling along the ground hoping I wouldn't step on a hot coal.

My mother and he would load the camels with our few little things. Women braided leather ropes out of animal hide and they were very strong. Mama tied the braided ropes under the camel's belly and from behind its ears to under the tail. She tied our things to the ropes. Then she coaxed the animal to kneel down so she could easily reach the animal's back. She put our blankets over the hump first as a base. Everything had to be tied tightly and carefully balanced so that it would not fall off or shift around during the long hike. It was hard to see in the dark and sometimes the whole load would come undone and my father would beat my mother for it with the bottom of his shoe. Mama loaded heavy things, like our milk baskets, on either side, and then added our cooking pot and smaller baskets. On another camel she fastened the mats that covered our round house, rolled up and tied on to either side. Mother built the load like a little house and made it comfortable for the camel to carry. In the middle you can put a young child or a baby animal that can't walk fast enough to keep up. We'd been told stories of children who didn't keep up and were left behind to die in the desert. We tripped and fumbled; scared to leave something behind, scared we might be left behind. My mother sang the work song or *salsal* while she and my father loaded the camels.

> *Nagging and worry are the companion*
> *Of a husband with many wives.*

I don't think my father liked that song but it was one all the women sang, so what could he say? After the camels were loaded, my family would walk all night and most of the next day. My people do not ride camels. Only a baby, an old relative or a sick person will ride on a camel's back.

I had to choose between moving out myself or putting up with Dana to see who would back down first. I went into my office, sat down in my chair and took a deep breath to calm down. This was my apartment; I paid the rent and the utilities every single month. In Somalia grievances are discussed and worked out by the men who are involved. There are no bosses; each man is given an opportunity to speak. A woman is not considered a member of her husband's tribe so her brothers or relatives will present her side when they are involved in a dispute. When my mother married my father she did not become a member of the Daarood because of the marriage, her alliances remained with the Hawiye. The men gather under a big tree and discuss the problem for as long as it takes to reach a decision that everyone can live with.

I didn't live in Somalia any more, I lived in Brooklyn where I had rights. But it turned out that since Dana's name was on the lease, he didn't have to move out. When I had found the apartment I was near my due date with Aleeke and I flew out to Omaha to have the baby near Dana's family. I was nervous about signing a big long legal paper like that. It's hard to read and I really didn't know what it was all about. So Dana stayed behind with my cheques and met with the landlord to lease the place for us.

A home is very important to nomadic people because our surroundings change frequently, but I looked around the place and decided, well this isn't a place where my soul is nourished anyway. I couldn't live somewhere with a dead spirit, a dry waterhole, an empty den. It was time to move on; the grass was gone and the place was full of *djinn*. There was trouble everywhere!

I knew that I needed to change myself – that I was a lot of the problem but I didn't know what to do. I have always been wary around men, not only because of my father, but due to other things that have happened to me. Many encounters with men in my life have been awful and I am guarded and suspicious. I thought it would be different with Dana because he was so shy and sweet when we first met, but I ended up feeling taken for granted. I thought I left all those lazy men who let their wives do everything behind in Somalia but I found the same thing in the West. Too many men have taken advantage of me and worse.

A friend of my father's came to live with us when I was quite young. He was called Guban. He stayed with my family during the dry season and didn't leave until the *gu* rains came. He came from Galkayo where he got into a fight with a man from another clan. Guban had a knife and almost cut off the other man's arm. Everyone in the clan is held responsible when blood is drawn so our clansmen paid the *diya* – the price to settle the dispute. They sent Guban to stay with us in the bush until tempers were not so hot.

Guban was funny and always teased me; he reached out long arms and secretly snatched at my *guntino*, my wrap-around dress, when I walked by. He looked at me right in the eyes. I loved it and thought he was a special person. One evening he said, 'Waris, do you want me to come with you and help you round up the lambs?' I was flattered that he was interested in me – a little girl.

Halimo said, 'Don't trust him,' but I didn't listen to her, she was always telling me to do this or that. We walked out into the bush – down the *tuug* and back up the other side to call the lambs as the sun slipped behind the end of distant hills. He found a pretty acacia tree and said, 'Let's take a rest here in the shade.' He took his jacket off and told me to come and sit down next to him.

There was something strange about him and I said, 'No, let's get the lambs and go,' but he insisted that I sit on his jacket. I sat down on the very edge of it and he lay right next to me. He was so close that I could smell his sweat. I watched the lambs for a while chewing on the grass and nuzzling the ground to get the good young shoots.

'Listen Waris,' he said. 'I'm going to tell you stories. Lie down and look up at the stars starting to come out.' I liked that and lay right down on the edge of the jacket away from him.

He turned on his side and faced me with his head propped up on his hand. He tickled my neck and told a story about a girl who had a big nose. He touched my nose, and then he said she had a thick neck and a big belly and big breasts. He fondled me every time he told me about the woman in the story. One minute I was lying next to him and he was telling me a story then he was pulling at my *guntino* and he grabbed me and untied the knots. He pulled me underneath him even though I yelled and told him to get off. Of course nobody could hear because we were so far away from the camp. He reached down and pulled up my dress and rolled over on top of me. His *maa-a-weiss*, the cloth he wore wrapped around his waist, was open and he pushed my legs apart and sprawled on top of me. He was poking my vagina with this thing and I screamed, 'Stop it, stop it! What are you doing?' He put his huge hand right in my little mouth and the next thing I knew he squirted something. He rolled off then started laughing and I had this sticky stuff all over me. I never smelled anything like that in my life and I still hate that smell, I hate that smell. I stood up, wiped myself and ran all the way home. I grabbed on to my mother's leg and smelled her – she smelled clean like the earth. I didn't know what to say because I didn't know what happened. I didn't know anything about sex. We never talked about it. That man did something wrong but I didn't know what he did. I couldn't explain in words so I just held on to my mother's leg.

She stroked my head and said, 'Baby, calm down, what is the matter darling? What's the matter? Did a hyena chase you?' I couldn't cry, I couldn't talk, I couldn't say anything. I just stood there – I couldn't let her go. I felt dirty and shamed but I didn't understand why. I hated that man because he did something bad to me, one of the family who helped him.

Breaking up with Dana didn't solve my problems. I was a single mother with no place to live and no family to help me. Getting him out of my life was supposed to help, but it only made things worse. The more alone I felt the more I wanted my mother. But my dream to find my family again seemed impossible. Only terrible news about Somalia made the newspapers. In October 1992 I read, 'Up to two million Somalis are said to be in danger of starving to death and already are dying at a rate of 2,000 a day.' There are only four and a half million people in Somalia so I believed the news reporters when they said, 'Somalia descended into hell.' I didn't know what had happened to my family in the years of famine and clan warfare since I left. I knew that the government had totally collapsed after Muhammad Siad Barre ran away in 1991. Almost ten years later a new government had not been able to establish peace among the warring factions.

My mother didn't even know I had a son; Aleeke was three years old and there was no way to tell her about him. What limited mail service once existed in Somalia had been destroyed and my family never lived by a post office. No one in my family could read or write so even if there was a postal service I couldn't send a letter or an e-mail, or a fax. My poor little country has not kept up with technology, it has gone backwards.

I was a person without relatives, as good as dead and gone.

3

bush telegraph

Good Fortune is riding on God's wing
On its flanks a good omen is in view
Regain your calmness my son and don't despair.

Somali Song

The phone rang one cloudy afternoon and I knew I had to answer that call. I just had a feeling about it. It was somebody calling for Oprah Winfrey. She is a powerful businesswoman and I respect that.

'We are putting together a program on sanctioned violence against women around the world,' the voice on the other end of the line said. 'We would like to have you on the show. Part of the broadcast will be on empowering women.'

'Do you want me to talk about FGM?'

'Female genital mutilation will be one of the issues we cover,' she said, 'but Calista Flockhart is going to interview women in Africa about that.'

'Calista Flockhart?' I said.

'She's the actress who plays Ally McBeal on television.'

'Oh,' I said, but I thought, what does she know about FGM?

If it wasn't FGM I couldn't imagine what I could say or why Oprah would want to hear anything from me.

'We would like you to do the segment called: *Remember Your Spirit.*'

'Spirit?' I asked, 'not FGM?' I didn't get it; I felt like an elephant trying to see its backside.

'Yes,' the woman said, 'we think you would be perfect for our segment on remembering your spirit.'

I was astonished that they didn't want me to do FGM. The last thing I had at that time in my life was spirit. I was a milk basket in a drought, all dried up with nothing good inside. I couldn't understand why Oprah Winfrey wanted me to talk about spirit and have a white girl who was never infibulated talk about FGM. What kind of spirit did I have to remember anyway? It seemed like everything I tried to do had dissolved in my hand like salt. I told her I would think about it and get back to them. My heart and mind were overflowing with troubles and problems I couldn't seem to solve.

That same week, very early in the morning, the shrill sound of the phone woke me up and I looked over at the clock next to my bed to see what time it was. It said five o'clock but I was still sleepy and I couldn't remember if it was five when the clock said five, or six. Maybe it was four when the clock said five. A friend had warned me about daylight saving and the time change but I couldn't get it straight – especially half asleep.

'Now why do we have to change the clock?' I asked him. 'How can time change?'

'It's fall back and spring forward,' he said. 'You set the clock back an hour in the fall because the sun is rising later and later. We want it to be the same time when the sun comes up.'

'Why don't you just get up with the light?'

In Somalia, nobody tells the sun what to do. Near the equator daylight is pretty much the same all year round and I could tell how long until sunset by the length of the shadows. What did clocks have to do with the sun? In Western cities there are so many lights that it doesn't make much difference whether it's night or day and it's so cloudy and polluted you can't see the sun most of the time. In Somalia the sun ruled our lives, when it was dark you slept; when it came up it drove you out of bed. He mentioned something about the farmers in Michigan getting up to milk the cows. Goats wake up when the sun rises, why don't cows in Michigan do the same thing?

I had a feeling that call was from somebody in my family. In Africa people joke about the bush telegraph. Communication happens without telephones or paper; there's a sixth sense I can't describe in English. Often you know that someone is coming, or someone is sick. In the West we have the cell phone, the fax and the answering machine. They are nice but I believe that as long as you are in touch with God, you are in touch. People ask me all the time, 'Do you have your fax on? I have so many things to send you.'

'No.'

'Well do you have e-mail?'

I tell them, 'I am a little bit behind with the technology in your world.' There are important ways to be in touch with those you love that have nothing to do with technology.

That morning when I stumbled out of bed and picked up the phone, I found it was my oldest brother, Mohammed, calling from Amsterdam where he lives. '*Nihyea*, woman,' he said and it snapped me awake. He needed money and I told him I would send it. Waking me up at five in the morning is typical of my brother. I love him but when he needs money, he doesn't keep quiet about it. Mohammed told me he had met some relatives who just returned from Somalia. Not only had they been there without trouble, they had visited family members who lived near our mother! They were going back and Mohammed wanted to try and get some money to her. In my family if someone has money, you share – that's the way we are.

Mohammed was raised in Mogadishu with my father's wealthy brother so I didn't really know him. This kind of arrangement is not unusual for my people. A family member who has money is often asked to help the children of poorer relatives. Even the ostrich lays her egg in another nest. The unsuspecting mother sits on all the eggs and raises the chicks. Sometimes you will see thirteen eggs in one nest.

When Mohammed and I were growing up, the military dictator, Siad Barre, had taken over the Somali government. He was quickly named *Afweine* or Big Mouth.He was eager to make changes in the country. Somali was not a written language because the religious people and the government could not agree on a script. Educated people favored a Latin script, but the sheiks insisted that Arabic letters were better because the Koran was written in Arabic. Siad Barre negotiated aid from the Russians and the Chinese and he wanted to please both countries. Chairman Mao told a Somali delegation to China that he favored the Latin script and wished that the Chinese had used it from the very beginning. The Russians were also in favor of the Latin script. Siad proclaimed that Somali would be written with Latin script. This resolved the dispute and Somali was written for the first time. The government declared a cultural revolution and insisted that everybody learn to read within two years. New schools opened in Mogadishu and that's where Mohammed studied in Somali, Italian and Arabic. Arabic is the language of the holy Koran, every student studies it; meanwhile the southern part of Somalia was once an Italian colony so most of the government papers were still in Italian.

As Mohammed grew up, the city fell apart. The schools and hospitals paid for with foreign aid were never built. The only thing that grew was the army. Siad Barre was Daarood and there were plenty of opportunities for someone from the Daarood clan with the military. The army had a big demand for *khat* and Mohammed became a *khat* dealer. *Khat* is a green leaf that secretes an amphetamine like speed. Originally religious leaders chewed it when they recited the Koran all day and night. Later older men sat around all afternoon and tore little green leaves from bundles of *khat* branches while they discussed issues and politics. They chew the leaves into a sort of paste and collect it on the side of their mouths until they have a big fat cheek. Eventually all of their teeth turn black from it. I could never understand what anybody saw in it. It doesn't taste good and it looks even worse; men have green juice dripping down the side of their mouth. Mohammed smuggled *khat* into the country from the highlands of Ethiopia and Kenya where it grows and sold it to the army.

For teenage boys in the military *khat* was hip. After chewing the drug restless soldiers became more and more agitated and less rational. For the first two hours the chewer feels happy but later depression, fatigue and distrust kick in but it's impossible to sleep.

After Siad Barre took power in the early 70s, I remember

my Uncle Ahmed came from Galkayo to check on his
camels and goats. He seemed agitated and talked to my
father for a long time. My mother and I were braiding rope
out of long strips of camel hide and we sat near enough to
listen.

'Siad Barre's soldiers are looking for young boys.'

'What do they want with them?'

'They will take any boy they find to a place where they
train them to be soldiers. Believe me, many boys are already
gone, kidnapped! There is going to be a war with Ethiopia
over the Ogaden territory they stole from us. I don't want
my sons to fight, they are too young. I am going to hide
them.'

'Where will they get the guns to give little boys? Who
would give a gun to a young boy?'

'*Afweine* is getting money from everybody! Italy, the
United States, Germany, Russia and China give him money
and he uses it to buy equipment for his army. He has the
weapons – he needs soldiers.' Uncle sipped his tea and spat.
'I have heard this from many relatives,' he warned. 'Young
boys disappear while they are out in the bush with the
camels. Soldiers kidnap them for the army and steal the
livestock too.'

After he left, my father and mother thought they would
dig a hole and hide my brothers. Eventually my father sent
the boys to live with relatives in the North, and taught me to
help him with the camels. I was proud and determined to
do a good job, usually only boys had the honor of caring for
the camels.

Every few days I took the camels to the well along a path
my father found for us. He could always find water even
when no one else could. Camels don't store water in the
hump; the hump stores a kind of fatty food, like a power bar,

that camels can live on. The lead camel knew the route and the rest ambled behind following the sound of her wooden camel bell. I carried a goatskin my mother had sewn into a flat bucket with a long rope to pull the water out of the well. One day my path was blocked – army tents and trucks were everywhere. My heart stopped because I knew that the soldiers would rape girls and steal any animals they found. I climbed up a little hill and crouched down to watch the soldiers wearing brown uniforms walking around with their long rifles and bigger machine guns on the back of trucks. I let the camels go and hoped they would eventually head towards the waterhole. I crawled on the ground, detouring miles so the soldiers would not see me. The camels arrived before me. I pulled up water for them and then spent a dark night crawling back to our camp in fear of those soldiers.

My rich uncle decided to move away from Mogadishu. He said the city was falling apart. 'People live by *baksheesh*, bribing, and finding ways to steal and loot,' he told my father. 'Mogadishu is full of *muryaan*, street children, with nothing to do but cause trouble.'

'Hunger-driven men with no honor will eat anything and do anything to get food,' my father said.

'They are people who have no home and no way to make a living. We left that city and I never want to go back. The government is just a bunch of people out for themselves. Ordinary people are not safe there anymore.'

The war with Ethiopia did come in 1974, and from then on Somalia was troubled by civil war and later by famine. By 1991, Barre's forces had been defeated and the opposition took control over parts of Mogadishu. But they failed to agree on who would be president and this resulted in yet more inter-clan fighting.

I ran away from home and went to London shortly after his visit. News about my family was rare and soon there was no word at all. In December 1992, just after I came to live in New York from London to further my modeling career, I saw the *New York Times* Sunday magazine. A friend brought a copy to me and I could hardly stand to look at the pictures. A famine in Somalia had killed more than 100,000 people. It was not due to a drought but because of the civil war that broke out when Siad Barre's regime was overthrown. Now there was no government and gangs who cut deals with other gangs ran the place. Nobody could grow any food and most of the animals were gone as well. The pictures were black and white photographs of starving people. The relief agencies couldn't feed those who were starving because bandits looted the food intended for women and children. The pictures showed crying children with sunken eye sockets and their cheekbones sticking out of the sides of their heads. A woman who looked like a broken old umbrella was crumpled in a heap by the road. I heard that one out of every four children died in those terrible years. Of course the people to suffer the most were the women and the children. There was simply no way to find out about my family. The newspaper said, 'The lucky ones are those who have died in this forgotten land racked by war, drought and famine.' I watched the TV reports about Operation Restore Hope and the increasingly desperate efforts to rid the cities of armed and lawless soldiers.

A million Somalis fled the country and my brother Mohammed was one of the lucky ones who escaped. He called me when he arrived in Amsterdam. I was so happy that he was alive I flew right over to him.

When I saw Mohammed I couldn't believe this stick

person was my brother. His lower lip was split right down to the bone from going long periods without water. His collarbones showed through his shirt and he had a hollow look like part of him was dead or like he was empty inside. I grabbed him and held him tight. 'Mohammed, what happened, what happened to you?' My brother looked haunted.

'They locked me up in a wire enclosure and I was held there in prison for months and months. They didn't give us enough water or food.'

'Why did they do this to you?'

'Waris, it was a crazy time. The soldiers were drinking, and chewing *khat* all day long. They chewed *khat* for breakfast, lunch and dinner. They had stupid arguments and shot off their guns for fun while they drove around the city.'

'*Hiiyea*,' I wondered what Mohammed had seen.

'In the early evening they are high and reckless and the officers suspected anybody who was sober when everybody else was drunk or high. If you even said, "Hey, calm down. There might be people over there," they would yell at you.'

'The army was used to enforce government decisions, no discussion was allowed. The government declared that women had the right to inherit property and many religious leaders protested that this was against Islamic tradition. Ten sheiks were executed right in their mosques by *Afweine*'s private troops, The Red Berets. Those who demonstrated against the murder of their religious leaders were slaughtered in the streets. Soldiers shot off their guns and raped women and little girls like it was a game.'

Over the next few days Mohammed explained how *Afweine* became suspicious of anyone from the Majeerteen, Hawiye or Issaq clans. He recruited clansmen from his family clan, the Mareehaan, for the SRC or Supreme Revolutionary Council and they did whatever he wanted.

One night my brother was accused of insufficient loyalty to
the president and sent to prison.

'They became suspicious of anyone from the Majeerteen
and one night they dragged me out of bed, beat me up and
then chained me in a dark room for over a week. No trial,
nothing – just punishment for nothing.' Mohammed didn't
really want to talk about it.

'How did you eat?' I asked him. He was so thin his eyes
were sunk into his head.

'They never fed us, we got a little rice and a cup of water
to wash.'

'Oh, my God, Mohammed,' I said. 'How did you get out?'

'Everybody was high or something all the time and Uncle
got enough money to bribe the guards so I could escape. They
knew that if I stayed in Somalia I was a dead man. Relatives
somehow got enough money for me to get out of Mogadishu
and put me on a transport to Kismayu on the Southern coast.
Afweine's clan was not so powerful there. From there I took a
dhow to Mombassa and a plane out of Africa.'

After all the horror he had been through my brother
remained connected to Somalia, even eight years after he'd
escaped. His early morning call to me came when I had
almost given up on the whole idea of going to Somalia, and
I do believe it was a message from Allah. It was a miracle he
called at just that time. If anyone could help me, he could.
He told me that my mother was living near the Somali
border with Ethiopia in a village where it was pretty quiet
and safe. My father now lived in the bush near Galkayo but,
even though he was still too proud to live in a village, he was
no longer a nomad. The constant warfare had claimed most
of his camels and he had trouble with his eyes. He lived
with the two wives he married after my mother.

'Mohammed,' I said, 'I have been dreaming of going back to Somalia.' My brother had heard me say this before and he didn't believe me.

'Yes, yea, yea woman,' he said. 'You ran away twenty years ago, how are you going to go back now? It's better to try and send them money.'

'No, Mohammed, this time I really mean it. I want to go home but I am worried and not sure how to go about this. Would you help me?'

'*Hiiyea*,' he assented.

Hiiyea? Like everybody else I expected him to give me a whole bunch of warnings about how dangerous it is and why would you ever want to go back there. *Hiiyea* means something like 'I hear you'. It was as if someone lit a match in the dark.

'Do you think it's safe enough to travel? Do you think I would find anybody that I know? I haven't even spoken Somali for years,' I said, anxious and excited at the same time. Back in 1995 I agreed to do a documentary for the BBC because they would help me track down my mother. I saw her for three days in Galadi in Ethiopia, near the Somali border. I didn't go into Somalia because of the danger. I'd struggled with the language then.

I was serious about going to Somalia; I wanted to go for it. Mohammed agreed to go with me if I would pay his expenses. He has a small stipend from the government and no extra money for a trip like this one. He speaks excellent Somali, useful for me in case mine didn't come back. I felt safe going with my brother and I could leave Aleeke with his wife and their children in Amsterdam. I decided to do it the very next week. News about the area where my mother lived could change and the door might close forever. When Mohammed said he thought we could also find our father the phone went sweaty in my hand. Just the thought of my father made me anxious even after all these years. Mohammed was also anxious about the trip. He barely escaped with his life, and memories of his vicious treatment in Mogadishu filled his dreams. It had taken him years to even get official refugee status in Holland and he was not allowed to study or to work. What did he have? The opportunity to wait. He was looking to find solutions for himself as much as I was.

That afternoon I called Oprah's people back and told them that I had to decline because I would be in Somalia while they were filming the show. I didn't want to pretend I was full of a beautiful spirit when I really had a hole in my heart.

Once I made the decision to go and find my family I was in a panic about it. The women in my family are proper Somali women, they don't wear tight pants and a T-shirt with a baseball cap. I had thrown away all the raggedy Somali dresses back in London like a caterpillar shedding its cocoon. Now I wanted my cocoon back. I hunted all over New York City, the garment capital of the world, but could not find any Somali dresses or *dirah*. These are floor length to cover the legs completely and made of a light gauzy material. The dresses have flowers or colorful geometric designs and are simply made. You measure four yards of cloth by holding it in your outstretched arm to your nose. Village tailors with foot pedaled sewing machines take the cloth, fold it in half the long way and cut a round hole for the neck. They sew up the sides leaving a few inches for the armholes, stitch the neck circle and put a hem at the bottom. Underneath you wear a petticoat. I didn't know anyone with breasts big enough to need a bra, especially me! Women cover their heads with a long scarf which is pulled over the face when going out or talking to a man other than your husband or father. Legs, however, are considered highly provocative and any women who would dare to wear shorts or tight pants would be stoned or worse.

I asked my friend, Sharla, and she sent me to Banana Republic. 'What do you have for the desert?' I asked.

'We have some nice cargo pants, khaki shorts, and safari hats.'

'I need things that are loose and flowing, no zippers, or waistbands,' I said. 'Pants are hot in the desert.' She showed me a long black dress and I asked if she had anything more colorful. 'I like colorful clothes, I don't want to look like the desert,' I said.

The only thing I could find were Indian saris. Some of the cotton cloth was similar and I thought I could make a *guntino* out of it though that really isn't what the women in my family wear. The sari material is much longer because it's wrapped around the waist under the little bodice, Somali dresses fall straight down from the shoulders.

I wanted to bring presents for everybody in my family, especially my mother. However, as soon as I started shopping I got stuck. What could I bring? Nomads don't have things just to have them and I had no idea what anyone really needed or wanted.

My family would not know what to do with tin silhouettes of the skyline of New York, or plastic models of the Statue of Liberty. My mother wouldn't appreciate a big pencil with a tassel on the end or a T-shirt with pictures of the Empire State building. They would only appreciate things they could actually use or eat. So I bought baby oil, cocoa butter and coconut oil because it's always good to have something for dry skin in the desert. I also bought combs, yellow soaps in the shape of a fan that smelled good, hair oil, toothbrushes and toothpaste. We used a tooth stick to brush our teeth when I was a girl and I wondered if my family could still find those special bushes that the sticks came from. We don't have dentists in Somalia and so I thought toothbrushes would be very useful. For my mother I bought the most beautiful mirror I could find. I wanted her to see herself, to see how beautiful she was. I walked up and down the aisles in the stores thinking, no, no, no. Food and water are essential, the animals are essential and travel is essential. Things are not important to my family. We don't use tissues, paper towels, disposable diapers, toilet paper or tampons or sanitary pads. When women have their periods they wear an old dark dress and stay in the house. We don't wear lipstick, face powder, eyebrow pencil or mascara. We don't have electricity for hair dryers, or toasters. I thought about clothes but nomads wear only what they have on their back. They don't have a closet full of different things to wear and I have never been interested in owning a lot of clothes myself. I like to model things, but I have never been interested in keeping them.

In the end I decided on colorful scarves for the women and sandals for my mother and father. We don't eat candy and food would be spoiled by the time I got there – so I forgot about bringing anything edible. I bought razors for my brothers so that they could shave. I bought my father a comb and brush set then I took it back to the store because he would hate it. He had always rejected me. I will never forget when he said, 'I don't know where you came from. You are not one of us.' How do you present a comb and brush to someone like that? All the tears I never cried because I had to survive were still there, trapped in my heart. But now I didn't have time to cry, I had a journey to make.

4

differences

Men protect one another's flank
Thus they become brothers
Shall we aid each other
Or part company?

Somali Working Song

To get to Amsterdam, the travel agent in the American Express office told me that I could buy a twenty-one day advance purchase or I could leave on Tuesday or Wednesday and return on Wednesday or Thursday with a Saturday night stay-over. I explained to her that my brother had found out where my mother was but that she might have to move on, so if I'm going to do this I have to do it now. The woman stared at me from the other side of the desk like I was very strange. When I came in I noticed that she had an enormous handbag on her desk. She took out a giant economy size bottle of lotion and squirted some on her hands just before I sat down. Why women walk around all day carrying an entire drugstore full of things they don't need is a

mystery to me. Somebody like that could never understand
a nomad so I said, 'I need two tickets for next week, one
adult and a child.' When she asked me about the dates for
our return, I told her, 'I'm going from Amsterdam to
Somalia and I really don't know how we are going to get
there and back but, God willing, everything will be OK and
we will get back safely.'

Her eyes got very wide and she said, 'I didn't know you
could go to Somalia.'

'I'm going to try,' I said. 'My mother is there.'

Her eyes softened and she nodded at me. She explained
that she had to have a specific return date and time or the
tickets would cost more. She also told me I might have difficulties with immigration if we had an open ticket so I
booked our return to arrive the day before I had a meeting
at the United Nations. I used a credit card to pay for the
tickets and told her I didn't want the clerk in the airport to
say he couldn't find something on the computer that I never
had in writing either. I wanted to have a ticket I could hold
in my hand and show to the person at the airport.

She laughed and confided, 'I feel the same way.'

We left on a Tuesday night and I called Mohammed that
afternoon to tell him what time to meet us. He still didn't
believe me and said, 'Really! I'll believe it when I see you at
the gate,' even though I assured him we were on our way to
the airport.

I was so proud of Aleeke on the airplane. He sat there like
a little man and looked at the people or drew for the whole
trip. My son likes to fly or ride in a car even if it means he
can't run around and jump on everything like he does all
day at home. When he had to go to the bathroom he got up
and walked down the aisle and into the little room as if he
did it every day. He is a traveling nomad like me.

Sitting next to him in the seat I could clearly see the top of his little head. He had a skin problem and I hadn't been able to figure out what was wrong. His soft fuzzy hair was falling out in clumps and I could see he had little white lumps on the back of his head. I had tried everything to get rid of them. I took pure oil of eucalyptus, added a drop of water, and rubbed it on the bumps. I pounded oregano into a paste to kill the germs and made an ointment of honey and myrrh. After I ran out of herbal remedies I took him to my pediatrician but he just said, 'Children get these all the time.' The doctor prescribed some white sticky cream but it didn't make any difference; the white lumps were still there. Here I was on my way to leave my child with someone I didn't know and he was sick.

Mohammed's wife, Dhura, and I had never met. I had last seen Mohammed when he escaped from Mogadishu and got to Amsterdam. He hadn't met Dhura then. She was also from Somalia. After talking to her on the phone for the last two years I felt that I knew she was a good woman and a caring person. She pushed my brother to do things and take care of the family. Once when he and I had an argument and we weren't talking to each other she told him to call me. 'Don't be stupid,' she told him, 'you are the oldest. Come on, call your sister – say hello – tell her the news from Africa.' I knew in my heart that she would be good to my son.

Just because someone is a relative doesn't mean that they will care for your children. When I was a girl, about up to my mother's breasts, I went to stay with an aunt. Unfortunately I got very sick the day after I arrived. First I was hot then I was cold and my head ached all the time and I was so weak I could hardly talk. Probably it was malaria. My aunt was not helpful – she just let me lie there while she went out to gossip with her friends. She told me to take care of her children even though I couldn't stand up without getting dizzy. I wanted my mother so badly I prayed for Allah to tell her. Mama knew what to do when people were sick and she made everyone feel better with the bark she gathered and pounded into a powder while singing special healing prayers. Sometimes a touch and a cool rag can heal as well as an antibiotic. My aunt didn't make any special teas for me; she acted as if she might catch my disease herself. I had a feeling about Dhura however, and I knew that she would take care of my child as if he were her own child. It was very important to me that Aleeke learn Somali ways. He wasn't going to learn them from Dana who didn't understand African thinking.

When I met Dana he was proud that I was from Africa. He thought I was special and exotic, later we disagreed over most of my ways of doing things. We had the same skin color, but we came from two different worlds. Dana is an African-American and he would say, 'Let's grab a slice of pizza on the way to the movies.' In Somalia we don't do that sort of thing – food is a gift from Allah. We wash and say a little prayer before we begin to eat. We eat with our hands and food is taken slowly and respectfully. It always offended me that Americans would push food into their mouths while walking down the street. Did Dana and I disagree because I was raised in Africa? Was it because I made money? Because I was well-known? Was it because of my modeling?

When I first walked into the club where Dana was playing with his band I knew there was something about him. I started to dance so that I could watch him. That night I was wearing a green sweater with high-heeled boots and I had my hair all wild in an afro. He told me, he couldn't take his eyes off the girl in the green sweater with the afro. Later I teased him, 'I am going to have your child.' He really got scared like I was a nut or something. When I was pregnant with Aleeke I reminded him of that. The very first time I saw that man something told me that he was the one for me.

Dana impressed me with his spirituality right away. He grew up in the Midwest and he was sensitive and shy. He struck me as an honest, good-hearted person. It's not easy for me to trust men and Dana's caution was magical. In addition to my infibulation, my earliest memories of sex between my parents are scary. One night when I was very little I heard noises I didn't understand and I saw my mother lying on her sleeping mat on the other side of our round hut. My father was on top of her. She didn't say anything but he pushed and sighed and grunted. I got up to see what was going on and went over to them. I reached out to get my mother's attention and the next thing I knew I was flying across the room. My father had grabbed my leg and pitched me up in the air backward. I was so stunned I didn't even cry out, it knocked the wind right out of me. My big sister, Halimo, took me in her arms. 'Be quiet, Waris,' she whispered. 'Leave Mama alone now.' When I asked my mother about it in the morning she shooed me away. Sex was a secret thing.

Dana was gentle and refreshing like rain in the morning. The more comfortable and safe I felt with him the sexier I felt. He would brush my hand and I would feel excited. I don't believe that infibulation kills all sexual desire, but it has made me very cautious, very reticent. However, once I feel safe and secure I want to be held and touched all over my body. My family and my people are very affectionate. Although men and women are never together in public, it's not unusual to see two men holding hands and walking together through town. Somali men express their friendship by touching in the same way that women do with close friends. In the West you only hug when you greet an old friend, so it felt wonderful to be physically close to Dana. Women who've had a breast removed because of cancer can still feel sexy. Part of my body was cut away but nothing important was missing when Dana kissed me. For me sex has to do with how I feel about my partner. An orgasm begins in my head and ends in my heart. I am easily spooked, but Dana touched me shyly and I fell in love with him.

After Aleeke was born our differences were more obvious. We don't use diapers on little babies in Somalia. Mothers are so close that they know when the baby is going to make water. You sit down on the ground and straddle the child over your open legs. The baby goes in the sand and you can use a leaf to wipe the baby's bottom. Allah's handiwipe. The whole time you talk to them and tell them what they are doing so they associate the action with what you are saying. When children start to walk it's easy to get them to squat down on their own and go by themselves. All of the little children just wear a T-shirt until they are three years old or so. They are very proud when they are old enough to wear shorts or a dress.

Dana didn't understand this and neither did his grandmother. She was the one who raised Dana and we visited her all the time. She felt that the child needed to be wearing a diaper at all times. I can understand that when it is cold out but around the house I let Aleeke go with just a shirt on as soon as he was crawling. Dana felt letting Aleeke run around without a diaper on was wrong. I think a little baby's body is beautiful and wonderful to see; children are so physically perfect. Dana's family thought it wasn't correct to allow a child to be naked. The comments they made were hurtful but I wanted to be accepted by Dana and his family so I dressed my son in shirts, pants, shoes and socks. However, I couldn't get over disposable diapers. What a waste! All that paper from so many babies just thrown away? Where does all that paper and plastic end up?

Even though Dana and I were not married when I had Aleeke, his grandmother, whom we both called Granny, never did anything but love my child. She was so happy to have such a great grandson. She reminded me in some ways of my own grandmother because of her self-reliance, strength and old-fashioned values. I guess she is a typical American grandma. My grandmother in Mogadishu was a very correct Somali lady. She never went out of her house without covering her face. 'How can you see in there?' I always asked her. She had to raise her children by herself and she did things properly. Dana's grandma's manners were very different to mine. She always questioned everything I did and how I did it. She didn't seem to want to know about African ways, she wanted me to learn her ways. Granny lived in Omaha, Nebraska all her life and she had never even seen the ocean. I used to joke that one day I would take her to dip her two chicken feet in the ocean and then she would understand my world.

I always dreamed of breast-feeding my children, even before I could take care of the goats. My mother breast-fed my brothers and me until we were three or four years old and she was having another child. In Somalia we don't have baby bottles and if we did, there wouldn't have been the spare water necessary to cleanse them. When my mother cleans her wooden milk bowl she rinses it out with fresh goat urine. Then she takes a glowing coal from the fire and sterilizes the inside of the bowl. She uses ashes and sand to scrub the inside of the dishes after they are used. My mother's breast was my only nourishment as a baby; it was both food and comfort. When I got older I watched my mother and the other women breast-feed and I wanted to try that too. I wondered what it would feel like; it looked nice and close. A baby sleeps with its mother and is carried on her back so that whenever it cries she can swing the baby around to the front to nurse.

One day when I was too small to see over the tall grasses, I watched my aunt's tiny baby while she went to gather some firewood in the bush. He was only as big as a camel's head and his arms and legs were still tucked up next to his body. The protective amulet he wore was almost bigger than his soft baby belly. He started to scream and I thought, let me try something. I wanted to see how it felt to have a baby suck at your breast. When I put him next to my flat little chest; he reached for it with his little mouth and made a circle shape with his lips. It was a bizarre feeling. At first he looked surprised that I was different than his mother. I pushed him closer to me so he could get a better grip. He tried but there was nothing to take into his mouth. He got really mad then and screwed up his face like a camel hissing. He arched his back away from my trick and started to scream. I couldn't get him to stop until I finally tied him on my back so he couldn't see me and he quieted down. I decided it must be easier with your own children.

One of my sisters died shortly after she was born. My mother's breasts were full of milk for her and they began to hurt. She tried to milk herself like a goat but not much came out. After a few days they were big and red and hot when you touched them. The veins stuck out like tree bark. My mother started to cry from the pain and I was frightened and scared. I had never seen my mother cry even when my father beat her. 'Mama,' I pleaded, 'let me help you. I can suck it out of you.' I sucked the milk out of her breasts and spat it out on the ground. I sucked and spat and sucked and spat until she felt better. It didn't taste like the milk I used to drink; it had a bad smell and an acid taste.

When I found out that I was pregnant I wasn't worried, not the least little bit. I had watched so many mothers and babies, I felt like I had been pregnant over and over again. When I was eight months pregnant I traveled to Spain for a photo shoot. Dana's family was horrified – like pregnancy was some kind of an illness. They didn't want me to jump on an airplane and go to Europe. But my mother and my aunts didn't stop working because they were pregnant, I had never heard of that idea. I wasn't afraid to work and I put on a baggy sweater and got on the plane. The pictures show a woman who is full to the brim with joy. It was a beautiful pregnancy; I loved my big belly and the movement within. It was a blessing to be filled with life, an honor that Allah would allow me to create a new family. I felt powerful and confident that nothing would harm me.

Every time I went to the doctor for a check-up he would ask, 'Do you want to know the sex of the baby?'

'I don't want to know that,' I told him. 'I have a feeling. I know what this child is going to be.' I knew the personality, what the baby would look like, and how he would see the world. 'Will this child have two legs, two arms and two eyes?' That was all I cared about. Every day I would pray on my life for a healthy baby. I saw the babies born to be buried when I was a girl. My mother wrapped them in white and Father buried them on a shelf until Allah took them. When Aleeke came out of my body into the world I knew my hunch was right. Aleeke is my little brother, Old Man, come back to life as a spirit guide. The moment he was born, when the nurse handed him to me, we looked at each other, right in the eyes. 'Oh,' I said to him, 'it really is you, Old Man.' Aleeke looked right back at me and I know he knew too. I don't know how to thank God for giving me such a gift and bringing my little brother back into my life.

We had Aleeke circumcised in the hospital a day after he was born. This is very different from female genital mutilation; that should never even be called circumcision – it's not. In males it's done for medical reasons – to ensure cleanliness. I could hear Aleeke crying when they did it but he stopped as soon as I held him. Despite my strong feelings about FGM, I knew it was the right thing to do. My son has a beautiful penis. It looks so good and so clean. The other day he told me he had to go to the bathroom. I said, 'You can do that alone, you are a big boy now,' but he wanted me to come and see him. His little penis was sticking up straight and clean. It was lovely to look at!

Sad to say, I didn't have much success breast-feeding Aleeke. He was a healthy baby but he didn't seem to get enough milk. He would scream and cry and I didn't know what to do. My breasts were so huge I couldn't believe I didn't have enough milk in there but he just cried and cried. He arched his back and pulled away from me. I couldn't think what my mother or my aunts did, it seemed so easy, they never had a problem. The baby just sucked as far as I knew. Granny and Dana both said, 'Give him a bottle, it's better for him.' After I hadn't slept for three days I gave him the bottle and he took it just like that. He was content and full so I had to give up nursing. Granny said, 'Formula is better for babies.' I didn't want to argue with her, I wanted my baby to have a happy smile and a full belly. Dead children are wrapped in white, the devil's color, the color of mourning.

When my mother needed to go to the bathroom or pray she would hand my baby brother to me or my sisters or my aunts. We don't have high chairs, or baby seats or play pens. That was one thing I couldn't believe! A caged child is like a trapped lion or tiger. I always held my son and sang Somali lullabies even though they made me long for Africa.

> *Father camel is walking*
> *Far, far away*
> *Don't worry Baby*
> *Allah will bring him*
> *Back to our tribe*

Sometimes I sang this one:

> *Father is traveling, traveling, traveling*
> *Auntie is traveling, traveling, traveling*
> *Brother is traveling, traveling, traveling*
> *When Father returns he will bring many presents*
> *When Auntie returns she will bring many presents*
> *When Brother returns he will bring many presents*
> *All for the good baby boy!*

I taught Aleeke to drink from a cup when he was two months old because that is what I learned as a child. I poured a little milk in a cup and sat him in my lap then pressed his two cheeks together so his mouth was open a little bit. I carefully poured a drop or two into his mouth. Granny said, 'No, Waris. It's too early for that baby to learn to drink from a cup.' Well, that is interesting, I thought, because he is doing just fine. But I let her take him and feed him with a bottle.

She saw me washing him in my lap with a warm wash-cloth and offered to show me how to give him a 'good bath'. Granny thought it was better to put the poor little thing in

the sink where you wash the dishes. Leeki got scared and
screamed when she put him down in that metal basin. He
threw his arms back and his legs out until I picked him up
and swayed with him back and forth.

After cleaning her children my mother used *subaq ghee* or
butter on the babies' skin. When Mama had enough goat or
camel milk she poured it into her milk basket or *dhill*. A
dhill is an elongated oval basket woven so tightly that not a
drop, even of sweat, could leak through. Outside, branches
bent into a U, surround it. Mama tied the top on tightly and
let it sit for a day or two until the milk was thick like yogurt.
She put a little blanket under the *dhill* so it could be easily
rocked. That whole day one of the children had the job of
rocking the *dhill* back and forth. When Mama came back
home in the afternoon she would open the little hole in the
top to test it. If milk came through the hole it meant that it
wasn't ready. If nothing came out it meant that the butter
was thick and done. Mama opened the *dhill* and collected
the clumps of *subaq* from the bottom and the sides. It is
wonderful butter! Then she would give us the milk that is
left to drink. Whenever my mother made *subaq* it was a spe-
cially happy day – usually there was not enough milk to
make it. You also use the *subaq* to fry meat and as an ingre-
dient in cooking. We put it on our pancakes and in tea. We
use it as a face and body lotion and in our hair. My mother
massaged it into the babies' skin to keep it smooth and soft.

One crisp fall day when I was staying with Dana's family, I
put Leeki on my back with a length of cotton cloth. He was
about two or three months old. It was a bit chilly so I had my
green jacket on too. When I carried my brothers and
cousins on my back they loved it and I knew just how to do
it. I used my headscarf because it is tightly woven like a bed
sheet but not as wide. Mine is bright yellow, with a green and

red African pattern. I bent over and gently put Aleeke on
the flat of my back. You hold one of the baby's arms under
your armpit so they won't fall while you tie the cloth around
you and the child. It goes over one shoulder and under the
other arm and you tie it right in the middle of your two
breasts. It's comfortable, it's not heavy, and you are so close
you can feel every breath the baby takes. I never could
understand how people put a little baby all alone in a car-
riage. Even before he was born, Aleeke's grandmother said
we would have to buy a stroller.

I answered, 'We won't be needing that.'

She looked very surprised and said, 'Well, what do you
mean? How are you going to go shopping and take the baby
outside for a walk?'

I said, 'I'm going to carry my child differently.'

She said, 'Listen Waris, take my advice, this is your first
child and you really don't know what you are doing. You will
need a stroller. You can't walk around carrying the baby
everywhere.'

I said, 'I understand how you do things, but we carry our
children in a different way.'

She got a stroller anyway, a huge gray ugly one. I hated it
so much I stopped using it a few weeks later. Not so much
because of her, I loved her, but because it was as big as a cow.
I felt funny pushing it in the street. There isn't a lot of space
in New York City and here I was taking up the whole side-
walk so everybody had to get out of my way. It was bad
enough shoving the thing up and over the curb but getting
inside the shops was impossible. You had to lean way over to
push the door open, then quickly drag the stroller in after
you. I always worried that the door might close and crush
my baby. There was no way you could take the subway, you
had to walk everywhere no matter how far it was. Then I had

to leave it downstairs while I carried Aleeke up to the apartment, leave him alone and rush back down to drag the stupid thing under the steps where people could still trip over it in the outside hall. That is a so-called convenience I can do without.

Anyway I came running downstairs that morning with Aleeke on my back. The habits of my desert childhood remain and I am always running even when I have no destination. His itty-bitty head was hiding under my jacket, I felt so fine. I saw Granny in the kitchen washing up the breakfast dishes and I said, 'See you later Granny.'

She called, 'Wait a minute. Where is the baby? You said you were going for a walk with the child. Where is he?' She came out into the hallway and stood there holding the dishtowel.

'He's on my back,' I said.

She honest to God could not believe what I was saying. I moved Aleeke under my arm to the front, and pushed my jacket open and said, 'Here he is.' He looked at her with a big, happy baby smile. The woman had a fit, she didn't know how the child was hanging there. She had never seen such a thing and she couldn't understand how the baby was so comfortable. She kept insisting that he was suffocating and repeating, 'I am begging you to take it off.'

I laughed a little and told her, 'We are going for a walk, I will see you later.' But it bothered me, I needed support and reassurance, not somebody telling me I was suffocating my child. I wanted her to ask me, how do you do that, not assume it was bad because it was African.

5

endless flights

Closest are the tongue and the teeth, and even they fight

Somali Proverb

The plane dropped out of the clouds and landed next to the gray flat terminal in Amsterdam and I smiled even though the day was dreary and dark. I could see a tall figure sticking up like a thorn in the crowd waiting outside the gate. Sure enough it was my brother, over six feet four inches tall. Mohammed was there with a friend and he had the biggest smile on his face I ever saw. His eyes are the color of Africa, dark brown and deep with secrets. When Mohammed first escaped from Mogadishu he looked starved – starved of food, of water, and of hope. Now he was not as thin, but he still had a haunted, hungry look about him. He had the split in his bottom lip from extended thirst and I don't think that scar from the prisons in Mogadishu will ever heal. Mohammed wore round glasses and he watched us coming down the hall like a camel waiting for water at a well.

It was good to hold my brother again, to hug him and to greet him in Somali. With wide-open eyes Aleeke looked up at his tall uncle. Mohammed grabbed him and put him high in the air on his shoulders. Aleeke shrieked with delight.

Dhura was standing at the door when we got to Mohammed's simple flat an hour's drive outside of Amsterdam. My sister-in-law was exactly what I expected, exactly the way I visualized her. She has a round face and eyes that shine when she laughs. She is tall like my brother; they make a good couple. Dhura was wearing a long Somali dress and her hair was covered by her headscarf. She reached for me when I came in the door and held both my hands when Mohammed introduced us. She linked her arm in mine and held me close while she showed me the flat and where we would sleep. I could feel her warmth and strength. Dhura is also Daarood and has two children from a previous husband, a boy and a girl. Her son's name is Mohammed. She followed Somali tradition and named her first boy after the Prophet. He is about eleven. Her daughter, Zhara, is ten and already growing tall like her mother. Dhura's first husband disappeared somewhere in the madness of Mogadishu and even his family didn't know where he was. One night a mortar shell hit the building where she lived and the entire side of it crumbled into the street. Dhura took her children and fled to Kismayu and from there by boat to the refugee camps in Mombassa. When she arrived in Holland she gave up trying to find her husband and divorced him. She announced it to the people in his clan and they agreed with her.

Both children had soft eyes and they stood shyly behind

her long dress. They peeked out at Leeki with big smiles. He ran off with them to play and didn't look back at me. I was so happy I almost cried. I wanted him to have a big bunch of cousins to run around with and cause trouble like I did when I was little. He joined right in as though he knew them his whole life.

Dhura and I sat down to have some cardamom tea together. 'I am worried about leaving Aleeke to go on this trip,' I confided.

'Waris,' she said patting my hand, 'he'll be fine with my children.'

'He's got some lumps on his head and they won't go away,' I told her. I called Leeki over and he let Dhura feel his head and pop one of the bumps so the pus came out. They didn't seem to bother Leeki, he just wanted to go back and run around with his cousins.

'My Mohammed had this,' Dhura said, 'and if it doesn't clear up in a few days I can take him to a doctor here in Holland. The medical care is free and the doctors are very nice to us.'

'Free?' I was surprised. 'I paid over a hundred dollars to the doctor in New York and the cream he gave me didn't help.'

'The doctors are free and we have money for food and the flat but Mohammed is not allowed to work because he only has an F-1 refugee status. That means we can only stay until things are better in Somalia – we are not considered permanent residents. We are waiting and waiting and I don't have much hope that he will ever be allowed to study or get a job. Mohammed doesn't really want to go back to Somalia to live.'

Oh, I thought. There is no salt in the tears he cries about Somalia.

The next morning when Mohammed and I left the house to arrange our flights to Africa I put on a long wraparound cotton skirt that could sometimes open at the front when the wind blew to reveal my legs. I had a sweater and my jacket on and I was wearing socks and boots because it was cold. As we walked out of the flat my brother looked at me sideways and said, 'You're going to wear that?'

I said, 'Yes. Why?'

'I don't like that skirt.'

'I can go back and put on my jeans.'

He rolled his eyes and groaned, 'No! That's worse.'

I stopped walking and looked him dead in the face. 'What is the matter?' I asked.

He said, 'Is that all you have to wear? A pair of jeans and that skirt!'

'Well, brother,' I said, 'we live in wintry countries. I don't know what you want me to wear. This is what I wear, these are my clothes.'

He sighed and fumed, 'We are going to a Somali office where they deal with plane tickets and travel to Somalia. You will embarrass me if you show your legs off like that. You don't have something else to put on under it?'

I said, 'You know, this is going to be some trip because you and I have already started and we hardly left the house on the first day. I am not going to act like a Somali woman, cover my body completely and not say anything. I see how you tell Dhura to do this, do that, but let's get it straight right now: I am not taking it.'

'Waris, you don't know how things are here,' he started to say.

'You shut up,' I said to him. 'I left home when I was young – I raised myself and neither you nor any other man is going to tell me how to dress or anything. I pay my own bills, and you are asking me for money all the time. I know that in Somalia the legs are considered the sexiest part of the body and are always covered, but we are in Holland, so adapt already.' Mohammed looked very surprised. I don't think any woman he ever met talked right back to him. His eyes were as round as his glasses.

Before I left New York I bought American Express travellers cheques because we were going so many places. I didn't want to take a chance and carry cash, so the first thing we had to do was go to the bank. I needed to exchange at least four grand. We took a train into the city and went to the biggest bank in Amsterdam. It was all white with big columns in front and a brass door. Inside there was a long queue to change money. When my turn came, I gave the teller the travellers cheques and my passport. This pale man with a thick neck and a red nose looked at me over the top of his glasses and said, 'Are these your cheques?'

'Yes, of course they're mine.'

'Could you just sign here for me?' he said and pushed a piece of paper over from his side of the counter. I signed my name and after he turned it over several times in his hand he said, 'No, I'm afraid that these signatures don't go together.'

'This is my passport; it's the same name and it's the same signature.' I had at least five thousand dollars' worth of travellers cheques still in my backpack and I asked him if he wanted to see the rest of them. Even though I never went to school or had a teacher show me how to write properly, I can sign my name correctly.

His neck turned red and he said, 'No, I will not authorize this transaction. You will have to go somewhere else to cash these cheques.'

'There is nothing wrong with my signature.'

He stared at me and slowly repeated, 'They don't match.'

I stood up very tall and replied, 'I would like to see the manager.'

His eyes got very narrow like he just walked out into the sun and he said officiously, 'I am the manager.' I knew that he was no manager and what he was trying to do.

Mohammed touched my arm and started to get up to go. 'Let's go,' he whispered. 'You see the signature doesn't match, let's get out of here.' When I didn't move he started to get nervous. 'The two signatures don't go together, don't you see,' he said picking up the cheques from the counter. 'Come on, never mind, let's get out of here.'

I couldn't believe he would give up so easily. 'Stop it,' I told him. I wanted to beat him up for being such a baby. I hissed under my breath, 'Do not speak to me in this way any more! I know what I am doing.' I turned to the so-called manager and asked him, 'Well, where do you suggest I go?'

The self-proclaimed manager said, 'There is an American Express Bank on the other side of town. That is where they will be able to check the authenticity of your cheques.' He told us to take this train to there and then another train over across this and walk six blocks, turn left, and in the middle of the block . . .

I said, 'We have to waste all this time running all over the place because you don't believe this is my signature!' He glared at me and when I didn't move, he started motioning for the next person in the line to come forward. Mohammed was already backing out towards the door. I knew I could either make a big scene or walk away. I realized there was nothing I could say to that kind of person so I just walked away.

All the way to the other bank my brother huffed and puffed that it was my fault. 'You just don't listen,' he grumbled. 'You should always watch and see what is going on. The signatures looked different.'

'Well it was a different kind of pen,' I muttered. 'I think I used my left hand in New York and this time I used my right.'

It took us a long time to get to the other bank because of all the trains and waiting each time we had to change. Mohammed was all over me the whole time but I didn't say anything. I think you have to stand up for yourself and not let people push you around for no reason, but I didn't want to start another fight and I knew my brother was not going to listen to me.

The other bank was a branch of American Express and they had no problem with the signature on my travellers cheques. The clerk took the cheques and asked me, 'How do you want the money?' That's all he asked. I questioned him about what happened at the other bank. He was surprised. 'Really! Why wouldn't they cash your travellers cheques? What was the problem?'

'I don't have any idea. Maybe he didn't like Africans.'

From there we rushed to this place where my brother said we could get a cheap ticket. Again I didn't ask why we were in such a hurry or anything. I just let him direct me around.

Mohammed took me to a Somali office where they had Somali music and maps and other things. I wanted to see what sorts of things they had but my brother's got no patience whatsoever. 'Sit over there,' he said, 'in case I need you.' I had never seen anything like it – because I had really never seen him in action. He paced back and forth, back and forth, talking to a friend of his and some other men. He never sat down – his arms were constantly waving at no big thing I could figure. He jiggled his leg even when he was standing. I couldn't watch all that agitation and went outside even though it was chilly and damp. Mohammed came out with his friend, Ali, and hurried us over to a nearby travel agent. The tickets cost about two thousand dollars each and I gave the cash to Mohammed for them. That was my job – hand over the money. We purchased plane tickets to Bosasso, an airport on the northern coast of Somalia. I asked if we could leave tomorrow and fly directly there because I only had thirteen days before I had to be back in New York. The ticket agent told me there are no direct flights to anywhere in Somalia; there is no such thing. He explained that we would have to wait until Saturday. We would take an early flight to London and we had a couple of airplane changes on the way to Bosasso.

There are only a few flights each week between Nairobi and Mogadishu and they are canceled if there is any fighting in the capital. There is no safe way to get overland from Kenya or Ethiopia into Somalia unless you are part of a refugee aid convoy and I had not been able to arrange anything like that through my contacts at the United Nations. Recently gunmen had attacked government officials on their way to a peace conference and nine people were killed. Mohammed had heard stories from refugees in Amsterdam about the dangers of traveling overland. There are *shifta* bandits all over the place and they have lots of guns and even bigger weapons. They prey on people trying to get out of the country – especially if they think they have any money. You either pay what they want or you will be killed on the spot. Mohammed's friends told us that this flight into Bosasso was the most reliable because the further north you go the less trouble you are likely to encounter. Mohammed and Ali insisted this was the best way to go and so I bought the tickets.

'How are we going to get from Bosasso to our family?' I asked my brother.

'We can hire a car at the airport and drive to Galkayo. Mama is living in a village not too far outside of Galkayo,' my brother said. 'I want to stay away from Mogadishu.'

Mohammed didn't want to go anywhere near Mogadishu. He didn't even want to fly over it. 'Those rag-tag army commanders in Mogadishu don't know the difference between a passenger plane and a military fighter,' Mohammed said. 'They shoot at anything if they are high or bored – anything except *khat* smugglers.'

'So what do they have to shoot with?'

'Waris, they have Scud missiles,' he told me like I was stupid or something. 'They are old and dangerous to begin with, and they are in the hands of desperate people with no training and crazy people telling them what to do.'

'Mohammed,' I asked. 'What happened to Mogadishu?' I thought it was the most beautiful city in the world when I was a girl. Hammawein, the original part of the city, sits on the shores of the Indian Ocean. I used to go and stand out on the sand at the edge of the sea and look back at the two and three story buildings all gleaming white in the moonlight. I had never even seen stairs until I went to Mogadishu. My uncle said it was more beautiful than Mombassa or Zanzibar. Of course, I had no reason to question him. Sultans who traded with China, Persia and India in dhows that went up and down the Indian Ocean built many of the houses. One house was called 'milk and honey'. The Sultan who built it was so rich he had milk and honey mixed into the mortar for the bricks. It was a light golden color and faced that blue, blue ocean. They said it would never ever fall down because of the mortar. My aunt told me that the top floor was a long hall with four carved wooden doors on either side and that

the Sultan kept the women from his harem in those rooms
and they could only be opened from the outside.

'Waris,' Mohammed sighed, 'most of the city is ruined.
There are piles of rubble where the buildings were and the
streets are full of burned out trucks and piles of rocks left
over from barricades. Soldiers would get high on *khat* and
go out and aim at a building with a grenade for fun, to see
if they could hit it. They liked to watch things fall apart,
those idiots.'

'Allah!'

'Everybody was so crazy from *khat* and drugs they didn't
know what they were doing and they didn't want to think
about it. The city would be quiet all afternoon while they
chewed the *khat* then the trouble started after the sun went
down. After the effects of the drugs wore off everything was
quiet again.' Mohammed's eyes were flashing and I could
feel deep anger and rage in this man. He looked old and
drained of joy when he talked about it. Something about
him was ended, finished. Maybe that was why I didn't see
Dhura's belly swollen with a new life, a child of Mohammed.

When we got back to Mohammed's flat I could hear
Aleeke in the back room running around with his cousins.
Even though they are much older he was right in there chasing everybody around. My son is completely a warrior little
boy, he is so very Somali and African. The word for a man in
Somali is *warrior.* Being with my brother reminded me of
what Somali men are, and I had one in my son. In the bush,
when I was growing up, men were either fighters or herders.
We consider the warrior to be the best, and my Aleeke is definitely a warrior.

I was afraid he would grow up to feel different and
alone like I did – that he would not understand the family
heritage he comes from. He is a member of a powerful and

important clan. I wanted to take my son home and to introduce him to my mother, his grandmother, so he would know more than my mother's name. Her personality, her relationship to life and her wisdom; that's what I wished he could know. How could he be proud of himself if he wasn't proud about where he came from? I wanted him to know his family in Africa but, at that time, I knew that there was no way I was taking my precious boy that I loved more than myself. I just hoped we would get there safe and back and that it would be a peaceful and successful trip. The more Mohammed talked about bullets in Mogadishu and bandits on the border with Ethiopia the more anxious and nervous I felt.

Enshallah, God willing, I'll bring Aleeke another time. I want my mother to see that Aleeke is the spitting image of Old Man, my little brother who died, in every way everything about him reminds me of my little brother. She wouldn't believe me though; I knew she would have to see it for herself so I wasn't going to say anything about it.

When I showed Dhura the clothes I packed we laughed about the problems I had finding anything to wear in New York.

'Mohammed would never let me wear that wraparound skirt,' she said.

'I thought he didn't want to go back to Somalia to live,' I said. 'Why don't you dress like the Dutch women?'

Dhura nodded and smiled at me. 'We'll see,' she said. I asked her if there were places to buy Somali dresses nearby. She said that the women made them and offered to lend me some of her Somali clothes to wear on our trip. One *dirah* had flowers in bright yellow, my favorite color. She handed me a slip embroidered in blue and silver threads for underneath and a flowered silk scarf that matched to cover my

head and face. I put everything on and Dhura announced
that I looked like a proper Somali woman – only my eyes
showed. I walked around the room and lowered the scarf so
she could see my smile. The long dress swished around my
feet and I almost tripped over Aleeke who ran in to see what
all the laughing was about.

As a girl I always battled with those long dresses. One night
my father woke us and said we needed to move our camp to
a fresh pasture. My mother and I rolled up the grass mats
that covered the curved frame of our house. She pulled the
frame poles out of the earth and loaded everything on one
of the camels. We strapped the milk baskets and water skins
on another camel. My father led the camels and the rest of
us followed behind herding the goats. We walked quickly
without stopping from the middle of the night until the sun
started to sink behind the blue hills. Finally my father halted
the caravan at a new little land. We knew we would stay there
until the moon was full again. The place was grassy and my
father said he knew a well that was not far away and
belonged to our clan. As soon as you stop you have to make
an enclosure for the animals so my father said to me, 'Waris,
we must go and cut brush to make a corral for the camels
and goats tonight.' In Somalia, it seemed to me that every
single tree or bush had thorns so I knew I was going to be
scratched all over carrying them with my hands.

My father used his long knife to hack down the trees and
told me to tear the branches off.

'Carry that pile back to where your mother is putting up
our house,' he said walking swiftly over to a thicket a little
distance away. The wind was blowing and my dress kept
catching on the thorns whenever I tried to grab the bushes.
I had to be careful not to rip it when I pulled it out of the

thorns because it was my only dress. As soon as he was out of sight I tucked my dress between my legs so it wouldn't catch and started carrying the pile of brush back to camp. My father called, 'Waris, wait for me,' and I knew he would not let me walk around with my dress up over my knees like that. I took a big thorn and scratched myself, and then I wiped the blood all over my face and arms and pretended that I was bleeding all over. When my father caught up with me he saw my bloody arms and face and said, 'What's the matter?'

I said, 'Oh it's all right. It's all right. I'm OK – but look Father, I'm already bleeding all over the place and you want me to carry these branches and walk back with this dress blowing out and catching on every bush and tripping me. I can't do this!'

He said, 'Well OK, keep the dress tucked up for now but don't let anybody see you like that. As soon as you are finished put it back down. Don't forget to put it back down and cover your legs, *Afdokle*.' That was my nickname, *Afdokle*, Little Mouth.

I said, 'All right, all right.' I was so pleased that I got away with tucking that dress up. I ran ahead of my father and leapt all the way back to our camp. What could he do? We both had our arms full of branches.

My brother Mohammed drove me crazy for the two days we waited for our flight. I could hear him shouting at Dhura, 'Bring me my checked shirt. Where is the case for my glasses?' He couldn't sit still for a minute. It broke my heart and made me angry at the same time. He paced all day long and kept coming in to ask if I was packed. The day before we left I was holding Aleeke in my lap and giving him a little drink of milk. Mohammed saw what I was doing but he said, 'Are you ready yet?'

I said, 'Hey, brother, listen *warrior*! You know what time the flight leaves? It's nine o'clock in the morning. We are going to sleep here tonight, you know. We got all night before we have to leave.'

'How are you going to get everything ready?' he asked. 'You have things all over the place.'

I said, 'I'm not packed, Mohammed, but I have most of my things ready and I'm not worried about it.'

'Don't take that,' he said pointing his finger at the duffel bag I brought from the States with all my presents. 'They don't need your garbage. We should only take certain things with us.'

I said, 'That is mine and I am bringing it.'

'Well I don't know how you are going to carry all that or get it on the planes,' he shrugged.

At five o'clock that night he had his brown suitcase all ready. We didn't leave for the airport until five o'clock in the morning but he was already packed and his stuff was sitting at the door. I went into the back room and finished arranging everything in my cases. At one-thirty in the morning I was packed. I tucked in my little Aleeke for the last time, stroked his head and sang a little song to him. 'Mama is going to Africa,' I sang, 'she won't be here when you wake up but she will be back soon.' He was sleeping so sweetly, I didn't know if I could bear to leave him. Sometimes in your life you just have to put one foot in front of the other. Before the next sun rose we would begin our journey.

I couldn't get to sleep that night and just as I drifted off Mohammed pounded on the door. I still had not adjusted to the change in times between Europe and New York and it really was the middle of the night for me.

'Get up, it's time to go,' he called.

'Hey, we got time.'

'Waris, we have to go,' he said, all upset. 'We have to get to the airport.' Mohammed was panicked about missing the flight for some reason so I got up and hurried into the car. We left my brother's house before five o'clock in the morning and drove for over an hour and a half through the sleeping city. We arrived two hours before we had to board the plane. I watched the sun come up through clouds the color of an elephant's hide and I prayed to Allah to bless us with a safe trip. We boarded our flight to London. As soon as the plane started to move down the runway Mohammed wanted to get up and go to the bathroom. He was suddenly desperate and started acting like a little child. The fasten seatbelt sign was on but he kept whining, 'I want to go to the toilet. I have to go to the bathroom.'

I said, 'Hang on for a second, Mohammed. The sign will be turned off any minute. As soon as the plane is in the air they will turn it off and you can go.'

He moaned, 'I can't wait, I can't wait!' rocking back and forth in his seat and wriggling all over the place.

Finally I told him, 'Well, if you really can't wait, then just get up and go. Go if you must go.' Mohammed started to get out of his seat but one of the flight attendants rushed over and told him to sit back down.

'No, no, mister,' she said. 'Sit down, you can't get up now.'

He sat back down but started crossing his legs and holding his stomach. I looked at him and thought Aleeke would do better. My son would just get up and tell the stewardess to get outta his way. My brother sat there moaning louder and louder. People started to look at us and I hissed at him, 'Hey, brother, you are embarrassing me, and you are acting like a child. If you have to go – just go. Pee on the bitch if you have to – but go.'

'They won't let me,' he whined.

'She has no right to do that – if somebody has to go, they just go,' I told him. 'Why are you listening to her?' She was treating him like some ignorant little man but why he waited until the last minute I do not know. Every time he got up she would look at him and he would sit back down. I couldn't understand why he let her tell him what to do.

At Heathrow airport we boarded a plane that took us all the way to Bahrain. After over seventeen hours of flying plus all the time between planes and getting to the airport I had no idea what time it was – where I was, or how long we had been traveling because of all the time changes. I was tired, annoyed and fed up with little seats, no room and terrible food. When we finally got off the plane in Bahrain I asked Mohammed how much longer it would be until I saw my mother.

'We are not even halfway there yet,' he told me. He got out the tickets and pointed to a section. 'We have to change planes again here and fly to Abu Dhabi.'

'Abu Dhabi? I didn't know we had to go to Abu Dhabi.' I had bad memories of that place. Our sister was there, but the last time I was there I had so much trouble with my papers that I couldn't go out of the airport to see her.

'Yes,' he said. 'But the flight to Abu Dhabi will only take another hour. From there we go to Somalia.'

On those endless flights my heart was filled with doubts. Who would I see? Who would be healthy? Who would still be alive in that home to battles, starvation, jagged rocks and whirlwinds? How would my mother accept that I never married the father of my son? A single mother with a child in Somalia is only one thing – a prostitute.

I wanted my father to see me, to look at his daughter right in the face. People all over the world have looked at pictures of my face. Photographers and magazines have paid a lot of money to take photographs of me – to capture my face on film. I wondered if my father even knew what I looked like. When I was a girl, all of his attention was for the boys. Girls were supposed to bring the tea and go away. I was never to speak to a man unless I was spoken to; I was barely allowed to stay nearby when the adults were talking. Now I had lived in a place where men and women talked directly to each other. I didn't believe that it was wrong or that something bad would happen to you or a *djinn* would be attracted to the trouble.

'Waris, look down when you are talking to your father,' my mother taught me as soon as I could carry a milking bowl.

'Why?' I asked, looking into her eyes.

'*Ebwaye, ebwaye!*' she repeated – shame, for shame. She said the same thing if I sat with my legs open or my skirt was up. She would never answer my questions, or give me any reasons. Why is it shameful? What does that prove or mean? That is the way things are in Somalia. When I was a girl I didn't like it; now that I had lived in the West, I hated it. I respected my culture, but I wanted to look my father in the eyes. I knew that he would never look away from me – he would expect me to look down, to demonstrate my respect for him. I was not going to do that! I was going to look right at him, stare at him, and hold his gaze with my eyes. He would see me, Waris, the daughter he sold to an old man for a few camels who now earned her own money. He would have to look at the girl he never sent to school who became a writer. The girl who was a United Nations special ambassador for women's rights.

FGM was another thing I wanted to talk about. My family's intention was not to harm me; it was something my mother and her sisters and her mother went through themselves. They honestly felt it had to be done in order for me to be pure. They believed that it was specifically ordered in the Koran. I know better now, this ritual practice is not even mentioned in the Koran, but that is not what they were told by the *Wadaddo*, the religious people. Nobody could read the Koran or the Hadith – my mother listened to the sheiks, she didn't question what she was told.

My father told me, 'Waris, you are too strong and wild. You have to get married now or no man will want you.' He thought that getting married would stop me from speaking out, from acting like a boy. The choice of a husband is not based on love. It is made by the parents to ensure support, tighten clan alliances and produce children. The price a man pays for the woman shows that he can support a wife. If he has nothing to offer and his clan will not contribute some livestock, then he has no connections and should not have the responsibility of a wife.

'She will bring many she-camels and white goats for her bride price,' my aunts always said about my older sister, Halimo.

'*Hiiyea*!' my mother would answer lifting up Halimo's dress to show off her legs when only women were present. Everyone would grab at her dress to tease her. She would whirl around and flash her sexy little ankles. 'This one will not go for less than twenty camels, I'll tell you that,' Mama bragged. She didn't pick up my dress to show off my legs. They had a funny shape and stuck out to the side. My legs weren't pretty but they were strong and I was fast. When you are taking care of camels you have to move quickly. You must take big strides or you will never get to where you have to go before it gets dark and the hyenas can see better than you. I thought my father would be proud of me because I could move as fast as any man, but I was always in trouble for talking back or tucking my skirts up. No matter what I did I was only a girl.

We always used to hide behind my mother when my father was angry. Once we moved our camp in the middle of the night, arrived in a new pasture and unpacked. My father sent me right out to watch the goats. I was so tired from walking all night long that I fell asleep in the shade of a tree. I was only a little girl and I couldn't keep my eyes open. When I woke up the sun had moved and I wasn't in the shade any more. One side of me was blistered black and the animals were gone! Gone! Terrified I looked for hoof prints but there were too many and I couldn't tell which way they went. Finally I climbed the biggest tree around and from there I could see little heads off in the distance in high grasses. When I ran to the animals, I jumped through the grass like a gazelle. Relieved to find any of them, I didn't even want to know how many were missing. I pretended like nothing had happened and went back to our camp.

My father counted every single animal in the evening before he put them in the corral and every morning before he let them out to graze. As soon as he started to count I stood behind my mother. He slowly counted those animals, *koe, laba, suddah, afra, shun,* up to fifty. The higher he counted the closer I stood to my mother. I wished I could climb inside of her. My father counted them twice but there were two animals missing, a baby sheep and a goat. He called my name, 'Waris, come over here.' I didn't move and he walked towards me. 'Did you hear me calling you?'

I said, 'Sorry, Papa. I didn't know you wanted me.'

He said, 'Come here.'

I knew if I went near him I would be crushed and there was no way I would move away from my mother. I said, 'No!' No one ever said no to my father. No one. I knew I was going to get killed anyway so I might as well take a chance – anything. I thought about running but where would I go?

My father grabbed a stick and Mama put her hands up and asked him to calm down. 'Don't beat her, she is just a baby. Let's just think about where the animals could be,' she said. In one split second, he hit my mother so hard it knocked her across the corral. She crumpled in a heap on the ground and blood ran out of her nose and mouth. I knew that if I didn't stay away from my mother he would kill me as well as her.

When my father was mad he reminded me of an angry lion. He had no mercy – nothing stopped him. Lions are like kings or queens. They sit there in silence all day and when they are hungry they kill gracefully, elegantly. They go directly for the muzzle or the throat and death is almost instant. Usually they are calm and dignified but there is one thing that they hate – being bothered, especially by hyenas. Once I watched a hyena tormenting a golden lion. He sat there quite calmly but all of a sudden, he had enough. He leapt up and in one single bound caught the pest in the middle of its back and crushed it. He shook the hyena in his mouth and threw it away.

I intended to go back and educate my father about what a woman could do – how a woman could make a good life for herself.

The minute we landed in Abu Dhabi my stomach turned into a big knot like we had come to a dry well after days of walking. I had such terrible memories of that airport and the United Arab Emirates. I hoped that nothing bad would happen this time, but Mohammed and I did not see any of our bags. We waited until the very last suitcase was picked up off the conveyer belt and I almost cried right there. I knew we had problems, and I was afraid of missing our flight to Somalia. First I thought that we had waited at the wrong place. Everything was in Arabic and I couldn't understand it.

'Mohammed,' I asked, 'are you sure that this is the right conveyer?'

'Yes,' he said, 'I saw other people from our flight.'

'Well, what could have happened to our things?'

'Let me take care of this.' Mohammed announced in Somali, 'I can deal with it.'

'Mohammed let me talk to them, I've been through this before, and I've traveled a lot.'

He insisted, 'No, no, I can do this.' He went to see a woman in a little office outside the baggage area. Waiting outside I could see that she was not in the greatest mood and he couldn't explain to her what had happened. She shook her head and pointed upstairs several times. I didn't think she had anything to do with baggage and certainly didn't know where our bags were. Mohammed got so frustrated that he started yelling at her in Somali and stormed out.

'Brother,' I told him, 'let me talk to these people, you are getting nowhere.' I went back to the office and the woman told me to go up to another floor and look for an information desk.

'We are looking for our bags,' I informed the man behind the counter when it was my turn. He didn't even look up or say anything to me, he just gestured over to another section of the airport. 'Excuse me,' I said. 'Do you speak English?' He waved again. I decided he could not help us and went to find someone else.

Another man in a little uniform said, 'Go talk to the agents at the gate,' so we walked all the way back up to the gate. The dress that Dhura lent me was too long and I kept forgetting to pick it up in the front. Every time I started to move I would trip – it was like being haltered. When we got back to the gate area the person just looked at us like we were crazy.

'Hey, wait a minute,' I said. 'They told us upstairs to come here for our bags. What is going on! I'd like to get some answers here.' He just shrugged and looked at Mohammed before he turned his back on us and began to walk away. I started to shout, 'Well what are we supposed to do? Just go with nothing? When are my bags going to get here?'

'I don't know when your baggage will arrive,' the clerk said to Mohammed. 'Go and sit over there.' He pointed to a row of hard wooden benches. 'Someone will let you know.'

Flights came and went. People walked by greeting relatives and picking up babies. Almost every woman was totally covered in a black chador, the men were free to wear whatever they liked. Some had pants and shirts, others wore traditional Muslim robes. The sun set and I saw it grow dark outside. 'Mohammed,' I said, 'check the tickets and see what time our flight is to Somalia. I don't want to miss that.' Mohammed got out the tickets but had trouble figuring out the times. 'Let me have the tickets, I'm going to ask someone so we don't miss that flight.' I pulled my scarf up over my head and covered my face. It was silk and would not stay on my head, it slipped off no matter how I tried to tie it. I took our tickets back up to the airline counter. 'We have been waiting all day for our bags and I need to know what time our flight to Somalia leaves. I really need some kind of information so we don't miss our connection.'

'There are no more flights to Somalia today,' he announced, still sorting through papers on the counter.

'Excuse me,' I said, letting my scarf fall down around my shoulders. I didn't care if he thought I was not Muslim. 'Did we miss our flight? Nobody told us, nobody will help us. What is going on?'

'There are no flights to Somalia today,' he said, still looking down.

I tapped the counter to get him to look at me. 'That can't be, there must be a mistake.'

'Let me see your tickets,' he sighed as if I was too much trouble. I handed him our tickets. He started flipping the pages and then pointed to the numbers in the little boxes. 'See here,' he sneered, 'you people left on September twenty-ninth and you don't get to Somalia until October second.'

'What?' I stammered

'Today', he said clicking the words slowly on the top of his mouth, 'is September thirtieth. Your flight is October second, and that is two days from today.' He made me feel stupid and small the way he kept pointing to the numbers on the ticket. He pushed them back to me over the counter as though I was unclean or something.

'Mohammed,' I cried, 'do you realize that we have to wait in this stinking airport for two days! I didn't know that!' He looked confused and anxious. 'These people are treating me like a fucking yo-yo,' I said. 'They won't even talk to me because I am a woman. Well excuse me, but I am a Muslim myself.' Mohammed looked over at me from the wooden benches with his hands between his legs.

I started to breathe deeply and when I finally calmed down I remembered our sister, Fartun. She works for a Saudi family as a maid and lives not too far from the airport. 'Let's get a cab and go to Fartun,' I told Mohammed. 'At least we can see our sister and have a shower and a bed while we wait for the flight.' We gathered up our things and I went to the bathroom and washed my face. I tucked my scarf around my head in yet another attempt to keep it there. Having my head and face covered all the time was miserable. What had I done to deserve that kind of punishment?

When we got to the passport control exit Mohammed walked right through. He has travel documents from

Holland and he didn't need a visa. However, a customs clerk with a nose like a hawk took my passport and started to go through every single page.

'You do not have a visa to enter the United Arab Emirates,' he said very slowly like he was talking to a child. I couldn't believe it. My mouth went dry, I felt like I couldn't get a breath. I had been through this.

'Please, please help me,' I pleaded. 'I am on my way to Somalia with my brother and I have not seen my family for a long time. Our flight does not leave for two days and I just want to go and stay with my sister until the flight.'

That man tapped on the passport with fat fingers. 'You don't have a visa to enter the country,' he said.

'I'm just trying to go home to my mother in Somalia. Can't you see that I am Somali?' His face was turned toward me but he looked at the wall. He would not look in my eyes. 'Please sir,' I begged. ' I just want to see my sister for two days.'

'You do not have the proper documents to enter the country,' he repeated. 'You can't leave this airport.' He practically threw my passport back at me. He turned and motioned for the next person.

I will never understand this need for documents and papers. Why do they have all this power over people; why do they dictate what people can do? Nobody has papers in Somalia. We don't need to show a passport when we are looking for grass for the goats to eat. If you want to see someone you go, you don't have papers to keep some people in and others out. You do what you feel, what you need to do. You are a person, not numbers and letters written on a piece of paper. It doesn't matter to a nomad where he is from, what matters is where he is. Once I asked my mother about the year that I was born – but she didn't remember.

'I have a feeling,' she said, 'I think it was rainy, but was it?'

I said, 'Mama, do you remember or not?'

'Please child,' she said, 'I don't remember. What could be so important about that?'

I have a feeling that I was born in the rainy season. You know why? I'm very much attached to water and especially to rain. I love it very much and so I have a feeling that it was rainy but I don't know what year I was born or how old I am. I do not know.

Nearly twenty years ago when I was about fourteen years old, my uncle decided to take me to London as a house-girl. He said, 'If I'm going to take you to London you'll need a passport, right?'

I said, 'Yes I do,' but I really had no idea what this passport thing was.

He brought me someplace where we took a picture and the next morning he had the passport. I didn't look at the writing, I only looked at my picture. It was the first time I ever saw myself. I was looking up at the sky in the photograph, I wasn't looking at the camera. I didn't know where to look so when the photographer said, 'Open your eyes,' I just looked up. (Actually I was praying to God because I didn't know what was going on.) I didn't realize what a passport was until years later when I was in London. My uncle just put a birth date on the passport that he made up. I still don't know what it was.

I left my brother in the middle of the crowd. I just had to move, to do something, to go somewhere. I went upstairs and found out there was a hotel in the airport.

'Do you have any rooms available right now?' I asked the agent.

'Yes, we do have a vacancy,' he said, 'but you have to pay

in cash.' He acted like I couldn't have enough money for a room.

'I want a room,' I insisted.

'They are $150 for the night . . . in American dollars,' he added like it was a dare or something.

God, I thought, I'm glad I have money. I checked in to the hotel and I didn't care how much it cost because I was so tired. It was a crummy little room, with cheap thin towels and a dirty brown cover on the single bed. I threw myself down and started to cry. I was worried about my little boy. I left him with some sort of infection to go on this crazy trip to nowhere. He had freaking bald spots all over his sweet head. I didn't know what it was and I wondered if God had been trying to tell me something. Perhaps God was punishing me. I felt helpless and trapped.

The airport in Abu Dhabi brought back a miserable memory and here I was again. I'd been sent back from this same airport; from the same place. I decided that it must be a curse or something. I don't know. I'd been trying to see my mother that time too. Mama had been caught in cross-fire between rival clans. She was out getting firewood, not bothering anybody, and soldiers started shooting at each other. She tried to get out of the way but she took two bullets in her chest. I sent money to Fartun and they brought her to Abu Dhabi for medical treatment. Of course I hopped on the first plane I could to meet her there. People in New York assured me that I didn't need a visa. When I arrived, after an 18-hour flight, they would not let me leave the airport. An ugly fat man said I didn't have a visa and could not enter the country. My mother and sister were right outside in the lobby but I couldn't get to them. I was so determined that I flew all the way back to New York and went to the United Arab Emirates Embassy and got the visa.

I spent another $2704 to buy a ticket back to Abu Dhabi. When I got back, the same heartless, ugly, short, fat man was there. He had two front teeth missing and I would have kicked the rest of his teeth out myself if I could. He took my passport with the visa stamp and left me standing there in the customs area. I waited and waited for the entire day. I was afraid to get something to eat or go to the bathroom in case he came back and didn't find me. Finally I heard my name called and when I came forward he sneered at me and said I was not allowed to enter the country.

'Please,' I begged him. 'I went back to New York to get the visa you said I needed. What is the problem? Please tell me. My mother was shot. She is waiting for me. Please let me see her.'

He looked at me and snarled, 'I told you. You will not be allowed to enter the country.' He handed me my passport and said, 'Where do you want to go? You are to leave on the next plane.'

'I am not leaving until you explain what the problem is.'

He said, 'There is a flight to London boarding at this time and I am going to put you on that plane.'

I told him that I didn't live in London. 'Why send me there?' I asked him. 'I live in New York.' I cried and pleaded with him but he wouldn't listen to anything I said.

'Do you see those women over there?' he snarled. They were very mean looking and wore police uniforms. 'Either you get on the next plane out of here or they will hurt you, I will tell you that. They will put you on the plane and they will hurt you.' Those women walked me through the gate to the plane and I could hear everyone laughing at me as I passed by. I will never forget it.

Here I was trapped in the same airport, paying over three hundred dollars for two nights in a crappy hotel room and being treated like I wasn't a human being. It got into my throat; my skin; my blood. I couldn't think of words in any language to describe it.

Islam means submission and a Muslim is one who has submitted to God. I got on my knees and said to Allah, 'Please help me.' I wondered if there would be something joyful and good after all of this aggravation. '*Enshallah, Enshallah.* Allah will work it all out,' I repeated over and over. There is a reason for everything; I truly believe that, deep in my heart, and I hoped to God it was a good one.

6

the night ride

Prayer against Evils
Evils lurking behind us, be ye halted there.
Evils waiting before us, be ye forced to flee.
Evils hovering above us, be ye suspended still.
Evils rising beneath us, be ye blunted of spear.
Evils treading beside us, be ye thrust afar.

Somali Gebei

Songs about Africa drummed in my head when our flight landed in my desert home after more than twenty years. 'Hello, Africa! How are you doing? I'm feeling good and I hope you are too,' I sang with a big smile as I stepped out of the plane and was greeted by the sky. I was home! I danced down the metal stairs onto the runway. My heart was pounding at the look of the land and especially the desert sky. The Somali sky is the home of the sun and the moon; it goes on forever, all the way into tomorrow. The sky is so big it makes you feel big too, not small. I stretched my arms out as far as they would go just to feel the space, to touch the freedom.

The sun is so bright and powerful that everything stands out – and everything looks close. I could see the Indian Ocean and it seemed like I could walk right over and jump right in. It had been such a long, long time since I had heard the sweet sound the wind makes over the open desert – I almost forgot about it. I knew the acacia trees, the beetles and the termite mounds, the tiny *dikdik*, the ostrich and the raspy sound turtles make. As we walked off the runway I looked at the people, I understood their faces – what they were thinking – what they were doing. After all those years of being a stranger trying to figure out what was going on and desperately trying to fit in, it felt wonderful. I could smell something and I knew immediately it was *angella*; it's what we have for breakfast. It is the opposite of sugary cocoa puffs, it's a sour pancake that fills you up for the whole day. Tears filled my eyes, but it wasn't sadness – it was joy. Mama Somalia, I thought, I've missed you so. How could I stay away for so long – you are so special to me. What kept me away so long? Everyone at the airport looked right to me, they looked normal and I felt a wonderful sense that I belonged. This is where my dreams come from. I am a daughter of Africa and I wanted to see my mother right away – then I would know that I was really home.

The sun was almost directly overhead in a clear blue sky and it was hot, very hot, unbelievably hot. After living in London and New York the intense heat caught me by surprise. Waves of warmth rose off the ground and it was hard to catch my breath. The Indian Ocean shimmered in the distance and I was glad there was a gentle breeze off the water because I had to get used to the torrid temperature. You have to relax in heat, you can't run around tense and excited.

There were no public buses or trains from that tiny airport. Men with vehicles for hire waited outside the whitewashed brick terminal along the road. Women own many of the cars. They worked as prostitutes in Saudi Arabia rather than starving to death or begging in the refugee camps. They bought cars with the money they saved and shipped them back to Somalia. They hired drivers and ran taxi services. Women in Somalia don't drive but if you own a car you are considered really wealthy.

Mohammed said, 'I'll handle this,' and walked up and down the row of cars and studied everybody. He saw a tribal relative he had known in Mogadishu and announced, 'There is somebody we can hire. Abdillahi is Majeerteen.' Majeerteen is our father's clan.

'Brother, let's make sure we get someone with a good car that won't break down somewhere,' I pleaded.

My brother had already decided. 'You can trust people from your own clan,' he informed me. 'Let's see if he will take us to Galkayo.'

Abdillahi had an old, beat-up station wagon. It was dented in the front and looked like the hood was wired to keep it shut. The tires were worn smooth as a baby's face and the seats inside were worn out and ripped. Mohammed greeted Abdillahi and the two men gave each other the double Muslim handshake and stood arm in arm talking. Abdillahi was tall with a thin face that ended in a little goatee. He wore a white shirt over the traditional maa-a-weiss. That's a length of patterned cloth that men wrap around their waist and tuck into a pleat at the front. It comes to about mid-calf length and most of the men at the airport were wearing them. Mohammed and Abdillahi went into the building to pay the airport tax and retrieve our papers. The stewardess had collected them when we got on the plane. My papers are British travel documents and they state that I am not allowed to travel in Somalia. I was frightened that they would send me back or detain me but Mohammed insisted that he could take care of it. The sun beat down until I had sweat dripping down the back of my neck all the way to my waist. It felt like it was over 200 degrees. What is taking these guys so long I worried. I was tempted to rip the silk scarf off that stuck to my head and neck and I couldn't wait to get into a car and get going.

Finally they came out and I could see that Abdillahi was upset. 'Your brother started a fight with the police!' he told me.

'They had no right to keep our papers. They have to give them back after I paid the airport fees!' Mohammed insisted.

'What happened in there?' I asked Abdillahi who seemed more rational than Mohammed.

'Your brother got upset with the clerk and started shouting. He almost knocked a policeman over when he pushed him out of the way,' Abdillahi said. Mohammed was still agitated and pacing back and forth. Abdillahi turned to him with his palms in the air, 'Calm down, you have to calm down.'

'They can't talk to me like that,' Mohammed continued. 'I paid a special fee and he has no right.'

Abdillahi waved his hand in front of Mohammed's face. 'This is not Europe, my friend. Those guys have guns and they use them. They don't care who you are or what the problem is – you have to stay away from trouble – don't argue with anybody who has a gun. It won't make any difference who was right if they shoot you.'

Abdillahi had grabbed my brother and dragged him back to keep him from hitting anybody. The police had returned my documents but I was frightened and afraid they might change their minds.

'Abdillahi, do you think you can find my mother?' I interrupted their argument about police tactics and soldiers on drugs and *khat*, eager to get out of the airport and find my family.

'Well, your family lives near the border with Ethiopia,' Abdillahi said. 'I just came from that region and I drove all night to get here for the plane. Believe me, I can find them.'

Still worried I inquired, 'Do you have a map?'

Abdillahi looked at me funny and said, 'I am Somali.'

'He can find them,' Mohammed laughed. 'He doesn't need a map on paper, it's in his head.'

'How long will it take to get there?' I asked, suddenly excited. I wanted to hold my mother, to touch her face.

'It will take eight or nine hours to get there depending on the condition of the roads and any military checkpoints,' Abdillahi said, stroking his little beard as he talked.

'What do you mean eight hours!' I screamed. I couldn't believe it. Three days of my precious time had already been wasted in airplanes and a nasty hotel room. Now I had yet another whole day of travel and the sun was already halfway across the sky. I was hysterical and paced back and forth, tripping on my dress. I ripped off the headscarf because it was choking me around the neck. It was so hot I couldn't breathe and I needed to move around, to get this trip over with. Eight hours in a car would actually mean two more days I would not see my family because we would have to allow a day to come all the way back to Bosasso to get the return flight. Mohammed and Abdillahi stood there looking at me like I was crazy or something. Time didn't seem to matter to either one of them. They lived on some other planet, not the one I lived on – the one with deadlines and appointments. I had no choice though, I had to just calm down and do what had to be done.

'How much will you charge to take us?' Mohammed asked. Abdillahi wanted three hundred American dollars for the trip. Mohammed offered him one hundred and Abdillahi refused.

'Mohammed, let's just do it and get out of here,' I whispered. 'Let's not waste time with this.' My brother glared at me like I should stay out of his business and I stepped back to wait in the burning sun while they bargained.

'Three hundred is not right,' Mohammed said. 'We are Majeerteen, you and I. My sister and I are not foreigners.'

'I am poor and I need money for my children.'

'Listen Abdillahi, one hundred American dollars is a lot of money, I know it, and you know it. It's more than the going price for this trip. Besides that,' Mohammed joked, 'you already know that I am crazy!'

'That's for sure!' Abdillahi teased. 'I guess I better get you and your sister out of here before you get in any more trouble. I'd have to contribute something to the blood price if you hurt someone.'

'Good, one hundred dollars,' Mohammed said and they shook hands on the deal. I gave Abdillahi the money to take us across the middle of Somalia to the tiny village where my mother was last seen. He looked intelligent enough and he seemed to know what he was doing but I wouldn't call him a considerate person; he treated me like men treat women in Somalia. It didn't matter that I paid for the trip. Both he and Mohammed left me to drag my duffel bag and all of our other things over to the car while they went to see some other relatives. I watched them hugging and holding hands as they greeted men they knew.

As soon as we landed in Somalia and Mohammed started speaking Somali he became an entirely different person. He stood straight and tall, his chin was up in the air and he was aggressive and cocky. It reminded me of the way he acted when I was a kid and he came to visit us. He showed up at our camp one day and started drawing things in the dirt.

'Hey you,' this strange boy called to me, 'are you ready to learn your abc's?' He acted like he was in charge and knew everything. I was curious and went over to see what he was doing. 'Sit down,' he ordered but I was afraid of the stick in his hand and so I stood to make sure I could get away if he started to hit me. He was making letters in the dirt but I didn't know that. I hadn't even heard of reading or writing. Mohammed was making *a b c d e f* very quickly with a big stick. 'What's this?' he demanded. Of course I didn't know what it was. 'So what is this letter?' he yelled at me, flicking his switch in my eyes. I didn't know what he was doing so I just stood there and stared at this crazy boy making lines in the dirt. He started to scream at me, 'You are a stupid nomad girl. What are you looking at me for? Look at the letters. Say them.' I started to laugh because he was shouting so much and I ran away when he tried to hit me with the stick. 'You bush people are too lazy and dumb to learn to read and write,' he called after me. 'Forget it, I'm not teaching you. I'm not going to waste my time with girls.' He threw a rock and it hit me on the ankle. After that I had a big sore and my mother told me to keep away from him. I was sure I didn't want any more to do with reading or writing.

Now he was strutting and acting like he knew everything and I was still an ignorant nomad girl. It was hot in the car but when I opened the windows too many flies got in so I stood there in the burning sun. Mohammed came back and ordered me to get in the car like I was the one who kept everyone waiting. He got in the front seat, I got in the back. 'You owe me for this,' he turned and said to me as soon as we were on our way.

I didn't say anything, I looked out the window at the country I longed to see. That is the way men are in Somalia. They don't listen to women and it doesn't matter who or what the woman is. You adapt to life in Africa, you don't change it.

There was a sort of petrol station on the gravel road that led away from the landing strip. Abdillahi filled up the tank and two large ten-gallon containers of emergency petrol and placed them in the back of the ratty old car. I was nervous about going so far with no map and no protection. I hoped we wouldn't have trouble with roadblocks or soldiers somewhere on the way. 'Allah, grant us a safe trip,' I prayed. 'Please help me to find my mother.' It was the *hagaa* or dry season and everything was brown and parched. Dust billowed behind the car and crawled in the windows and settled on every surface, fold and indentation. The road started out bravely, it was even paved for a little while, but it turned into dirt tracks. Tire ruts wandered off in other directions. I hoped that Abdillahi knew which tracks to follow and that he could keep the car moving over deep sand drifts and boulders fallen or thrown into the path.

We hadn't gone very far when Abdillahi turned off the road near several small huts. 'I have to get some *khat*,' he said, 'I drove all night to get here and it will keep me awake.' People were sitting in the shade but ran towards us with *khat* branches in their arms. Green leaves on twigs, demon twigs, I call them. Devil leaves. I hate the stuff and believe it is ruining my country. Now here it was the first thing I saw when I got back. *Khat* doesn't grow in Somalia so all the money men spend to buy it goes to Ethiopia or Kenya. Abdillahi drove slowly past everyone and looked at the small bundles of twigs and leaves they showed him. He didn't like any of it and drove on. Ragged little boys without shoes puffed on cigarettes. They weren't more than six or seven years old and they were smoking the damn things. With arms and legs as thin as toothpicks, they looked like spider children. When they are hungry they chew the *khat* so they won't feel it. Abdillahi stopped again a little way up the road where the same thing happened. Little boys and old women ran towards the car with bunches of *khat*. He waved to a woman with branches wrapped in her *chalmut*. 'Come over here Mama, come here,' he called out the window. 'How old is this?' he asked her. 'Is this new? Is it fresh? Is it today?' *Khat* loses its potency after a day. There are many airplanes that fly *khat* into Somalia and smugglers never have problems getting a flight with fresh *khat*.

'Well,' she said, 'we had a bad drought but, yes, this just came from Ethiopia last night.' He ran his fingers through the leaves, examining and studying them to determine how old they were.

'Hey, Abdillahi,' I said. 'Just grab a tree, man. Let's go!'

'This is pretty good stuff,' he said. 'Why don't you give her twenty shillings for it.'

'No,' I said. 'I'm not paying for your *khat*.'

'It helps me drive, and we have a long way to go. You know, I've been up all night driving to meet the plane this week. *Khat* will keep me awake.'

'I already gave you a hundred American dollars. What do you need that stuff for?'

He said, 'You are not going to get there for another two days unless I drive you. I know the roads. I know where to find your family. If we have any trouble with police or soldiers I will give them some *khat*. That's all they want, drugs.'

I told him, 'I am not paying for that shit. You buy it yourself.'

Abdillahi backed down and purchased his bunch right

there to start the journey. He put it on the seat next to him, near the steering wheel and gave it a little pat when he put it down. He tore off leaves one at a time and shoved them into his mouth. He chewed them into a paste then carefully tucked it deep into the side of his mouth so he could chew more leaves. I knew that in a few hours his cheek would be bulging and green juice would drip down his chin. He would be high and full of energy. He had a little tape recorder and turned the sound up as loud as it would go. All afternoon Abdillahi sang along with the Somali songs, the *gebai.*

> *He who has lain between her breasts*
> *Can call his life fulfilled*
> *Oh God, may I never be denied*
> *The well of happiness.*

Abdullah's voice was high-pitched and shrill. He could only sing out of the corner of his mouth in order to hold the wad of *khat* in his cheek. On and on he sang:

> *When fate decrees that evil days*
> *A tribe shall meet,*
> *Even the clouds must flee the path*
> *The cursed ones take.*
> *Faltering the elders grow, and weak,*
> *And counsel fails.*
> *As a vessel is overturned to shield*
> *Sweet ripe dates,*
> *So from the tribe's eyes God conceals*
> *Wisdom and light.*

Suddenly the music stopped. A bad pothole had blown out the front tire. Abdillahi pulled the car over to the side of the road. There was no traffic at that point other than an occasional truck so there was no one to help us. While shoving *khat* leaves into his mouth Abdillahi found a jack and changed the tire as if he did this every day – all day. It was incredibly hot in the car and I got out to watch. There was no shade and nothing to do but watch him jack up the car, push leaves in his mouth, take off the flat and put his spare tire on and more leaves in his mouth. If we blew the spare we would have to sit there until someone came by to help us – or rob us – or worse. Abdillahi tried to avoid the big ruts in the road but it was the middle of the day, the hottest time and heat was rising off the desert like steam. He thought that the heat as much as the pothole had blown the tire. As soon as we came to a village he stopped and bought another tire. They would patch the one that blew and sell it to the next people who needed a tire. Allah what a waste of time! We changed at least four tires on that endless trip. We drove for over fourteen hours and had to stop constantly. Abdillahi probably spent most of the hundred dollars I gave him on tires that day.

Distance in the desert is nothing. You can see so far that it feels like it takes forever to pass anything. Except for the plume of dust following the car, it doesn't seem like you are moving. The road was rough and I was thrown back and forth all over the seat every time the car hit another rough spot. I felt that road, I was a part of every up and down in that landscape. We traveled in three dimensions – forward, up and down. We traveled through space as big as your mind, nothing was hidden or secret.

All day my heart was heavy because of things we saw along the way. Children, no taller than a camel's belly, stood by the side of the road wearing rags and looking hopeless and lost. Where were their parents? I saw men whose teeth were black from chewing *khat*. Once when we stopped to change a tire a silent old man stood and watched us from the top of a little hill. He never moved, he never swatted the flies that walked on his eyes. I looked for the lines of camels, beautiful golden brown camels, the ships of the desert. But we only passed ragged people without animals. The worst thing I saw was a thin woman with a child on her back out in the middle of nowhere. She waved at us for a ride. It was getting dark and we had not passed a village for hours. She only had the front half of a shoe. The heel had broken off and her feet were torn and bleeding. They looked like a camel's feet, with deep crusts and thick skin, not like they belonged to a human person. I couldn't stand it and I pleaded, 'Please stop. Stop for the sister. Stop for the mama!'

'What's the matter?' Mohammed asked.

'The entire back of her sandal is gone!' I said. 'Her feet are bleeding from walking barefoot.' Once I had feet like that – so hard and deeply cracked they looked like a mud hole in a drought. She obviously had a long, long way to go and soon it would be dark. The hyenas would be after that child for sure. Sometimes you have to sleep in the desert at night because it's too far to get where you have to get. It reminded me of running away from my father when I was all alone in the desert with the dust and flies for company. When I ran away from my family I had to spend many nights alone in the dark with no food and nothing to protect me. I was scared to death of falling asleep because I knew that hungry things were waiting for the night. A lion waited for me and I woke up to the smell of his breath in my face. 'Please stop,' I pleaded. 'She can sit back here with me. There is plenty of room here.'

Abdillahi just passed her by, saying, 'Don't worry.' He flicked his wrist and passed her like she was nothing. Both men kept saying, 'She's a woman. What do you need to pick her up for? She's used to walking.' I was almost in tears but they would not listen to me. All day long we passed women and little children, leaving them to choke on our dust.

Mohammed had heard through tribal relatives that my father might now be alone in the desert. Three rainy seasons ago our younger brother Rashid was herding my father's camels near our tribal wells in the Haud. He was just minding his own business and he sat down in the grass to rest with the animals grazing all around him. Suddenly he heard a noise and he stood up. The next thing he knew bullets were flying everywhere. He started to run and several men chased him and shot at him wildly. Rashid was hit by a bullet in the arm and collapsed into the grass and passed out. When he came to, all the animals, my father's entire herd, were gone. The desert was silent except for the empty wind. My father's life's work, the animals he raised from a single pair into a major herd and kept alive in times of drought and little food, his fortune, his property and his pride, had completely vanished. Rashid dragged himself back to our camp and my mother took care of him. Fortunately the bullet went right through the bottom of his upper arm, right through, and didn't even hit the bone, so he was all right, but my father was crushed. My father disappeared after that happened. We have a saying that a desperate man will look in a milk basket to find his camels. His lifeblood was gone and the spirit went out of him. He sat with his head in his hands for days then wandered off in the night, nobody knew where. They didn't know if he went to search for his livestock and to kill the men who stole them or was in such despair that he had given up and was just looking for some place to die.

7

mama

In the name of Allah, the Beneficent, the Merciful . . .
Show us the straight path,
The path of those whom Thou has favored;
. . . not the path of those who go astray.

Koran, Sura 1, The Opening

We traveled on and on towards blue hills on the horizon but it felt like we would never get there. The sky stretched out in an enormous circle above us; there was no end to it and no end to the heat either. Abdillahi said it was hot enough to kill people if they didn't get out of the sun. Every bush and hill reminded me of my childhood, and especially of my mother. I was one of those children who was obsessed by her mother. I prayed every day that nothing would happen to her and I followed her everywhere, even if she didn't know that I was following her. Mama was my world and I don't know how I ever got the courage to leave her. I guess I never really thought I would and now one path had led to another and another and I had lost her. In Somali we have a word, *nurro*, it means instinct. Animals, and those who escape death, have the gift of *nurro* from Allah. It is how the termites build a home out of their own saliva, it's how a lizard knows to break out of its egg and find something to eat. I wanted to believe in my *nurro*, but I worried that I had been away too long. I didn't know how to read the signs any more. Maybe after this whole long journey we would not be able to find my mother at the end. It was all I could do to keep from crying with fear and frustration. Perhaps she was lost forever.

Night came as dark as a snake. I was discouraged and exhausted from the heat and from bumping and breaking down continually across those dirt tracks. Abdillahi worried me. What if he couldn't find the village and we were just lost, hopelessly lost. Without any warning he left the road and drove over a little hill. He turned off the engine and silence surrounded us like sleep. I could see a little encampment but there were no lights in any of the huts. Then Abdillahi announced, 'We're here. This is it.' Suddenly I was excited and full of energy. I jumped up in the back seat.

'Really! Are you sure? Is this where my mother lives?'

'Yes, Waris,' Abdillahi said, 'this is the place.'

'Thank you Allah!' I said. We had actually made it across the width of the country. Nobody had bothered us, only the heat and the tires had caused trouble. I got out immediately and leaned back on the car and smelled the air. Allah, how I love that smell. What is it? It's home.

Abdillahi pointed to a square house at the edge of the silent village and said, 'Your family is there.' He and Mohammed walked over and started knocking on the door. After a few minutes it opened and a tall man holding his *maa-a-weiss* around him answered. Mohammed said it was a cousin, Abdullah. He knew exactly where everyone lived.

He walked with us down a little street to another tiny square house. He knocked on the wooden window shutters and a pregnant woman answered. She stood in the doorway and stared at us with sleep in her eyes while Abdullah explained who we were.

'Who are you?' I asked.

'I'm your brother Burhaan's wife, but he isn't here,' she said. 'My name is Nhur.' When Mohammed explained that I was here to find my mother she quickly grabbed her scarf and took my hand in the darkness. She led us across a little path. The only sounds were our footsteps on the packed dirt.

Ahead of us, I could just make out the shape of a tiny hut. It was a one room shack made of upright sticks held together with twine and covered with bits of tin for a roof. We stopped in front and I took a deep breath.

'Wait a minute,' I asked my brother and Nhur. 'Don't say anything until I give her a hug and a kiss.'

Of course there were no locks. The door was just a thin sheet of tin fastened on to the side with pieces of wire for hinges in the top and bottom corners. The battered door leaned against the house and I had to pull it up and drag it across the ground to open it. My mother's house was so small that her feet were right next to the door and I bumped them when I opened it. My mother sat up and asked the shadows, 'Who's that?' I couldn't see anything but I crawled over the floor towards the sound of her voice. You had to bend way over to get into the hut, but Mohammed is so tall he bumped his head even though he ducked. That made another noise and my mother called again, 'Who is it?' I didn't want to say anything, I knelt there in the silence because I wanted to feel the moment. She called out, 'Who's that? Who is that?' Finally I found her head and I held her face in my hands and kissed it and then put my cheek next to hers so she could feel my tears running down my cheeks. She listened to my breathing for a moment, drew my face right next to her and whispered again, 'Who's this?'

'It's me, Mama. Waris.'

I could tell she recognized my voice, she kind of stopped breathing for a moment. Then she grabbed me and held me next to her like a baby snatched at the last second from falling into the fire. 'Waris? Is this really my daughter Waris?' she said and started to laugh and cry at the same time.

'Yes, Mama,' I said. 'It's really me, and Mohammed, he's here too.'

She reached up for him and held his hands and I felt her joyful tears on my arm. 'Where did you come from? I thought you were dead. Allah! Allah! My daughter, my son!' All of a sudden she snapped back and started rocking me back and forth and pretended to scold me, 'Allah – Allah! Waris, do you want to kill me! What are you doing creeping up on me like that!' Then she started laughing and crying again. 'You go right back where you came from,' she said. 'I'm too old for this.' Then she hugged me again and said, 'What are you doing here, child!'

I burst out laughing. She hadn't seen me for about five years, not since my short visit to Ethiopia, and now when I suddenly showed up in the middle of the night she could make a little joke. I thought, I hope that I have a little bit of my mother in me.

'Mohammed,' my mother said hugging him. 'I should have known it was Mohammed *Dehrie* when I heard you bump your head.' *Dehr* is my brother's nickname, it means the tall one because he stands as tall as a standing camel's head.

My mother was sleeping with a child but he never woke up with all our talk. 'Who is the little boy?' I asked.

'That is your brother Burhaan's oldest child, Mohammed *Inyer*, Little Mohammed,' Mother said stroking his sleepy head.

Abdillahi said he would take my brother Mohammed to sleep with my Uncle Ahmed and his family because there wasn't enough room for everyone to sleep in the tiny hut. Little Mohammed slept on after they left and my mother lit the little lantern we call a *feynuss*. It gives a soft light and I could see her dear face, her perfect nose and her eyes the color of cinnamon. She pulled me close as if I might be a dream and she had to keep touching me or she might wake up.

Nhur joined us and sat with us as we talked for a little while. Nhur said she had heard a car then voices of people she didn't know outside her house. That is what woke her. She hugged me and stroked my arm and dress. I told them all about our journey and how long we had been traveling. My mother rocked back and forth and hugged me and laughed in amazement as if we'd come on a magic carpet.

'Nhur,' I said, 'I am sorry for asking who you were. First of all, I didn't know you existed. I didn't know you were around! I didn't even know my brother was married the first time. I certainly didn't know that you are his second wife and already have a daughter and another on the way.' I felt embarrassed but – it's the way life is in Somalia.

Nhur patted my arm and said reassuringly, 'Really! I'm married to your brother for a long time now – and you didn't even know I existed.'

'I'm sorry,' I said. 'My hopeless brother Mohammed doesn't tell me anything.'

Nhur laughed again and teased, 'That means you didn't bring me any presents.'

I said, 'Yes, that's right and I am sorry.' I didn't have

anything for her, no baby presents nor anything for her little girl. I pointed to my bag and said, 'I'm sorry I didn't bring you anything but whatever you can find in this bag is yours.'

'What happened to Burhaan's first wife?' I asked.

There was a long silence and my mother said, 'She is with Allah in the garden of paradise.'

'I'm sorry, I'm so sorry,' I said. 'How did she die?'

'How do I know?' Mama announced firmly. 'It was her time and Allah took her.' Whenever you ask a Somali how someone died or passed away they say, 'Do you think I'm a God? God knows that, I don't know what happened.' That is all there is to it, when it's time to go, it is time to go. The Somalis believe there is a tree on the moon, the tree of life. When your leaf falls from the tree that is the moment that you will die. When you're dead, you go to heaven and good-bye. Death is between you and Allah. I knew that nobody was going to tell me what happened to that child's mother. My mother had taken in her grandson without a single thought; she saw somebody who needed her and she took him. He was about three years old and I could see that she was totally in love with that little boy. She was cuddled right up with him on the bed. He slept peacefully, soothed by the sound of her voice.

Mama looked like Mama – the person I knew all my life. She has skin like oiled ebony and when she smiles she is missing one of her front teeth. I think she lost it when my father beat her once, but she would never say. She has been through a lot and her skin is etched with lines of both wisdom and hardship. She didn't look old to me, the wrinkles around her forehead give her a great dignity. It tells you that hardship is not the same as worries.

Suddenly I heard drumming and pounding on the tin

roof. I jumped and said, 'What is that?' For a second I didn't know what it could be. It was so hard and so loud, and it didn't start slowly, it came all at once.

My mother and sister-in-law both laughed and said at the same time, 'Oh it's rain, Waris. Rain at last.'

Mama looked up and said, 'Thank you, Allah.'

Out of nowhere, it poured. In Somalia, rain is not the annoying little drizzle of the West, it's like a slap in the face. The rain really hits you on the head. It was drumming on the tin roof like dishes thrown on the floor.

'Oh Mama, it's going to cool down, because of the rain. It's really some beautiful rain.'

My mother looked at me in the lamplight. 'Child it hasn't rained for more than a year,' she said.

'Oh Mama,' I said, 'Mama, I brought the rain, I brought it.'

She clicked her tongue on the top of her mouth in disapproval, 'Waris, you are not God, so take that back. Don't you even say that – don't compare yourself to God. The rain came because Allah sent it – it doesn't have anything to do with you.'

I said, 'I'm sorry, I'll stop.' It was good to be reminded of the order of things in my mother's home. I was grateful to have that rain, I felt blessed by Allah himself.

My mother smiled and said, 'I knew you were coming.'

I was surprised at how certain she was. 'How did you know that?' I asked.

'I had a dream a couple of days ago about your sister. She was getting water and bringing it to me strapped on her back. She was singing the watering song and her voice got louder and louder. I knew one of my daughters was coming, but I didn't know which one it was.'

I sighed, 'Oh Mama.' My eyes filled up with tears because we are still so connected after all these years and all these troubles. What I missed more than anything else is the natural power and spirit that I used to know. I knew that I had to come back more often, I had to keep in touch with the powerful spirit in my mother's house. God willing, I would never stay away so long again. Now I knew the routes and how to get around.

My mother. I don't really know her – I was just a kid when I left, but I feel her, you know, like when you know something but you can't really put it into words. The last time I saw her in Ethiopia I begged her, 'Mama, come back with me to New York. I'm going to give you everything.'

She looked at me and asked, 'What do you mean, child? What is everything? I have everything that I need right here.' I felt, deep in my bones, that desert life was not right for me, so I ran off. Now I wanted to understand her life, to find her spiritual treasures and I never wanted to be without them again.

'Mama,' I said, 'do you know where my father is? Mohammed said he wandered off after his camels were stolen. And how is Rashid?'

'Oh, you heard about that trouble. Rashid is fine. The bullet went right through his arm, not like the ones that got stuck in my chest. Your father was determined to get his camels back but most of them were all gone. Probably shipped to Saudi Arabia or the thieves ate them. He finally gave up and came back. He's out in the bush, out that way,' she waved in the darkness.

Nhur explained that my father lived with another wife not too far from the village where we were. He insists on living in the desert with a few of the animals he did manage to get back. Each animal was clearly branded with his sign so, with the help of some tribal relatives, he was able to claim some of his livestock back. She thought maybe he had

about five camels, some goats and a few sheep. My youngest
brother, Rashid, was helping him to take care of them. I
thought about all the empty hills we had passed on our journey here and I wondered if we would be able to find Papa.
My mother still loved my father, but he had taken a second
younger wife years ago when I was young. He lived with her
in the bush most of the time. 'I heard that he had taken a
third wife too,' I said, wondering what my mother's reaction
to that had been.

'Well he did, but she ran away or he divorced her a while
ago,' my mother stated.

'What? What happened?'

'Child, I don't know why she left. Maybe she didn't want
to work,' Mama said flatly. The lantern started to smoke
and she reached over and adjusted it. We say that billowing
smoke tells secrets, but my mother's reaction to other wives
remained a secret. Often another wife is a blessing because
there is a lot of work for women and they can help each
other. However, my mother was not going to talk about my
father and his wives any more than she would talk about
what happened to Burhaan's first wife.

'Your father was operated on two days ago somewhere in
the bush,' Nhur whispered. 'Burhaan heard that it was bad
and went to look for him.'

'An operation in the desert?'

'*Hiiyea.*'

'Two days ago,' I gasped. If only we had been able to get
here sooner. I thought of that terrible room in Abu Dhabi
and the days we wasted there. 'What kind of an operation?'
I stuttered.

'His eyes, Waris,' Nhur said, softly. 'He was having trouble
with them.'

'Allah, his eyes.' I had heard that he was having trouble

with his eyes, but I just thought he would get better like he always did. I assumed he had a little vision problem and maybe needed glasses. My father needed me but I had not been there to help him.

'We heard that he was blind and in terrible pain,' Nhur continued. 'Burhaan decided to see if he could find him and get him all the way to the nearest hospital in Galkayo. We don't know what happened yet, but I hope he is all right.'

Suddenly I was crazy with worry and fear. An operation in the middle of the desert? Who would do that! How could anyone do that? I couldn't believe it. How could he find his way around if he was blind? How could he take care of his animals or find water? From Nhur's description I suspected he had cataracts caused by years of blinding sun reflected on the sand. 'I am going to see if we can find him tomorrow,' I said. Even if it meant another endless journey, then so be it.

When I said, 'Mama can three of us share the bed?' she replied that we would not all fit. She only had some cloths spread out on a mat and a ragged piece of mosquito netting barely big enough for herself and Mohammed *Inyer*.

When I was a child we used to sleep outside under the stars because it is hot in the houses with no big windows to capture the air. Outside, there is usually a little breeze after the sun drops down over the edge of the world and the stars come out. What I really wanted to do was fall asleep outside with just a few little sheets. However, the mosquitoes could be fierce after the rain.

After the rain let up I went to sleep with my newfound sister-in-law. I shared a sleeping mat with Nhur and her little girl. The three of us shared it every night that I was there. My niece is almost two years old. Burhaan's house is square and made of whitewashed mud bricks. There are two rooms and a third that is not finished yet. The walls are about waist high and when it is completed I hope that my mother will agree to live there. Mama preferred to live in the ragged little stick thing she built with her own hands. She has lived all of her life in houses she built.

That night I was tired after such a complicated journey and emotionally exhausted from all my worries and fears but I couldn't fall asleep. I was excited that I would see everyone in the morning; I couldn't wait. I lay down next to my sister-in-law and her little daughter and waited for my mind to stop whirling. Listening to the last drops of rain drip off the roof I felt peace settling into my bones. We found my mother, I knew my father was alive, even if he was in a hospital, and I had relatives all around me.

Suddenly I thought I felt something and then I saw a dark shape on my leg below the knee. I was lucky I even saw this huge shadow, because it was very dark. I stared at what I thought might be a scorpion for a long time. Then I slowly whispered to Nhur, 'Is that what I think it is?' I tried to stay calm and not move, because we had been taught not to panic. Danger will snap at you so quickly that you will never know what happened to you. So we know not to move. Maybe the scorpion is just passing you by – you never know. You may think you can get him off faster than he can sting you, but I knew that you do not move before you are sure that you are really in charge. So I stared at it in the inky darkness and I said again, 'Is that what I think it is?'

She whispered in my ear, 'Oh, yes.'

We call it *hangralla*, scorpion. When it turned around I knew from the pointed poison tail – without a doubt – that it was a *hangralla*. He was the grandpapa or mama of them all. He'd come to welcome me home to Somalia. I jumped up and mashed it.

Even after that, I had no fear as I lay back down to sleep. I pushed away all my worries, all my stress and chaos. I let the Somali darkness and the deep silence surround me. People insist that Somalia is one of the most dangerous places in the world but I was at peace. It was a peace I have not felt anywhere else in my life.

I never slept more comfortably. Actually I feel quite comfortable on the floor. If you roll, you are going nowhere. If you kick, you can't break anything. It's good for the back too. I hadn't slept so well in years. Things in New York keep me up, or I wake up worried about something. When you know something, and I know the ways of the desert, you know that you are safe. You can let your fears go and slip away from your mind like water spilt on dry ground. I slept soundly every night I was there. I really did. I heard hyenas laughing in the distant hills like a wicked, wicked woman. Ha-ha-ha they tease each other. But we are not afraid, you know why? We know they wouldn't come. They aren't coming to the village to snatch people. God's hands are covering the village, keeping everybody safe so you don't have to worry about tomorrow or yesterday.

8

desert dreams come true

Liver with blood

2 cups blood
500g. liver
2 spoons *subaq ghee*

Wash the liver and cut into small pieces. Put the liver, blood and *subaq ghee* into a small pan and cook slowly over glowing coals, stirring all the time. Do not fan the coals or the ashes may get into the food. Simmer until the mixture is tender and moist.

That morning I woke up in a different world. The dusty gray plain had turned into dark red earth with big puddles all over the place. Everything in my mother's house was soaked. I looked up and you could see the sky through the uneven parts of her corrugated tin roof. It wasn't like someone built her a roof; she had picked up scrap pieces of tin here and there and placed them on top of the branches she tied together to construct the four walls of her one

room. It was so small she had to sleep diagonally. Both she
and Nhur had been up before the sun. Nhur had already
been to the market and Mama was hanging her few little
cloths on the fence of thorn bushes surrounding the house
and on a rusty blue oil drum to dry. A battered truck tire
leaning against the house had water inside and one of the
goats was happily lapping it up. It looked at me out of the
corner of yellow-brown eyes and kept drinking.

We don't feel miserable and complain that stuff gets wet
when it rains, we say thank you to God. According to the
Koran everything alive is made from water. Rain means that
the grasses will turn green; the animals will fill their bellies,
and so will we. In the desert water is precious; it's blue gold.
We wait for the rain; we pray for the rain; we wash with the
rain. Without rain there is no life. We don't have winter and
summer, we have *jilaal*, the dry season and *gu*, the rainy
season. In Somalia, a guest is greeted with water; it is a token
of welcome and respect. I felt like Allah had offered me a
greeting. The difficult journey, the long hot drive, and the
hard days of drought were over; the *gu* rains had come and
Allah blessed us with water. It started my visit to my family
with joy and happiness.

I gave my mother a hug and kissed her good morning.
'God be with you, Mama,' I said. 'I am so happy to see you
and to be here with you this beautiful morning.' I grabbed
her and started squeezing her tightly. 'How I missed you! I
love you so much Mama, I can't tell you how I love you!'

'Ohh,' she groaned, 'you are suffocating me.' She looked
at me sideways with a wisp of a smile on the two ends of her
mouth. She pretended to be annoyed but her eyes were
shining with pride and delight. 'Waris,' she said, 'what a surprise to see you. I heard that you were dead. Somebody said
that – then somebody said you were a prostitute. Now Allah

brought you back and you are standing in my house, really I can't believe it.'

My mother has a special way of looking at life and it always catches me. She wears a string of black beads around her neck and a protective amulet. It is a little leather pouch with holy words from the Koran sewn inside. A *wadaddo* or holy man made it especially for her years ago and she never takes if off. It keeps her safe and protects her from evil spirits.

'Let me show you the presents I brought you from New York, Mama.'

She waved me aside with long expressive fingers and said, 'Go and see your uncle first.' That was so like my Mama, not to be at all interested in herself but in everybody else.

I knew from Nhur that my father's brother, my Uncle Ahmed, was not well and I needed to see him. Nhur said he had a *djinn* from the spirit world take over the left side of his body. I certainly didn't believe that. My uncle is older than my father – he could have a whole lot of things. When I was a child I watched after his goats for him. I remember that the thing I wanted most of all then was a pair of shoes. Now that I saw my home as an adult I understood why. Jagged rocks stuck up everywhere. How I remembered those rocks and thorns on my bare skin. Some thorns were so long they would stick right through your foot. When I was a girl I liked to leap and run; I had so much energy I couldn't stop moving. My feet were cut and bruised all the time, especially when I climbed all over the place after those goats. I envied their little hard hooves; nothing tore at their feet. My feet throbbed at night and bled all the time. I begged my uncle for a pair of shoes as payment for taking care of his goats. I watched his animals every single day and kept them safe. When it was hot and dry I had to take them off to distant places to find something to eat. Often I didn't get back until after dark and that is when I really tore up my feet. To this day I am obsessed with feet and shoes – it's the first thing I notice about people. I don't have a lot of clothes; I really don't care about them, but I love shoes. I buy comfortable ones though, not high-heels. They feel just like you are standing on rocks! Now why would you do that if you don't have to?

Finally Uncle Ahmed had agreed to bring me a pair of shoes from Galkayo. I dreamed about my wonderful shoes and felt they would be like a magic carpet. I could go anywhere without hurting and run as fast as the ostrich do, throwing stones up behind them, or leap like the gazelle when they get the scent of a lion on the prowl. When my uncle finally came I danced for joy, and whooped and shouted, 'Shoes, shoes!' My father yelled at me to quiet down and leave the man alone but I would not go away, I was too excited. Uncle reached into his pack and handed me a pair of cheap rubber flip-flops, not the sturdy leather sandals I expected. I was so angry that I threw them in his face.

Nhur had built a fire and the tea for our breakfast was steaming. She had found some liver in the market that morning and had already cooked it for my mother. 'She can't eat many things because those bullets are still inside her,' she explained to me. 'Mama keeps throwing up.'

'She is too thin,' I agreed with her.

'I hope the liver will build up her blood,' she said, and carefully placed the bowl on the ground for my mother to eat. Mother sat down in front of it and started to say a prayer over the food. Mohammed *Inyer* danced in. He was hungry and wanted some of the liver. He is too little to wear pants and he squatted down with his bare behind right in front of my mother.

She looked up from her prayers and said calmly, 'Child, move your bottom from my breakfast.' I was still laughing when Ragge, my Uncle Ahmed's son, walked in.

My mother greeted him warmly then reminded me to see my uncle. 'You better go,' my mother warned me, 'or your uncle will think you are favoring my side of the family.' Ragge was a little boy when I left and I remembered taking care of him for my aunt. Now he was about twenty-two, tall and slender, and he spoke excellent English. I liked him immediately. He had an old-fashioned haircut, short around the side with a longer piece on the top. He carried an afro comb in his back pocket and every five minutes he was running it through his hair.

Ragge walked with me through the village to show me the way to his house. There were maybe sixty houses with one or two rooms in various stages of completion. People had cleared the desert brush and built basic shelters. Families who had enough money to buy building materials inhabited the best ones. They had walls of sun-dried blocks and roofs of corrugated tin. Other women had patched together huts out of whatever they could find: old tires, woven grasses and bits of tin. Some of the houses were square and fashioned of sticks, others were round Somali *occles* made of the long roots of the acacia tree, arched and covered with woven mats and pieces of plastic sheets. Old plastic bags stuck on the outsides of the houses fluttered in the wind. Nothing that was lightweight and might be useful was thrown out. We passed a house with the mats folded back to dry out the inside from the rain. Other dwellings were round with baked mud walls and thatched conical roofs. Different clans built different kinds of houses. None of the huts had running water and there were no sewage pipes or electricity lines or even plans for such a thing. Someone had built a little hut for the chickens. It was round with a little cone top and a reddish hen was sitting inside clucking at me to leave her alone. A little boy not more than two years old followed us. He was free to go exactly where he pleased – he was perfectly safe walking all by himself. He had on a T-shirt and nothing else. His teeth were gleaming white against his black face and his shy smile was as wide as a camel's mouth.

It was exactly the life that I remembered from my childhood so many years and experiences ago. The village reminded me of the tortoise. It draws its head and arms and legs deep into its shell and refuses to acknowledge you even if you poke it with a stick. It will simply wait until you get bored and move on, and then will continue on its journey without changing direction. This village had nothing to do with what happened in the rest of the world. Nothing much had changed since I lived here, but I certainly had. When I was a child I felt like I had every single thing that I needed, except sandals. I didn't have any idea that I was poor. I still find it hard to believe that Somalia is one of the five poorest countries on the planet. The morning sounds of chickens and crying babies and smells of wood smoke and wet mats in the village were waking up parts of me that I hadn't heard from in a long time. It felt wonderful to be there but at the same time I noticed that none of the children had shoes.

My uncle lived with his daughter Asha and her husband in a square house made of sun-dried mud bricks and a corrugated metal roof. The door was painted a gay blue and decorated with a big red diamond in the middle and smaller dark blue ones on either side.

Uncle Ahmed was sitting next to his house on a *michilis* or a short three-legged stool made of stretched hide. His hair was white as a goat and he wore the traditional checked Somali *maa-a-weiss* wrapped around the waist and tucked in with a fold in the front. His hat was round with a flat top. It is the kind often worn by men who have completed the prescribed *hajj* or trip to Mecca to pray.

'*Afdokle*! *Afdokle*,' Uncle said, rocking back and forth. He called me by my nickname, Little Mouth. 'Sit down, sit down next to me. Let me look at you. Oh my God, child. Don't you eat? You are so thin – are you sick?'

'No, Uncle,' I laughed. 'You don't have to have a big behind following you to be healthy.'

'Well,' he said, 'you look terribly thin to me. Are you hungry child?'

I said, 'Yes, Uncle. We just arrived here last night and I am really desperate for *angella*.' I could smell it when I got off the plane and that is the very thing that woke me up that morning; the wonderful smell of *angella* cooking. To make this sorghum pancake, women pound the grain in a tube hollowed out of a log and grind it into flour. Before they go to bed they mix it with water and beat it to make it smooth and full of air. As night falls throughout the village you can hear everybody beating the batter. It's a competition because the louder the sound the better it is. In the morning the batter has risen and the women build a fire and put three large stones around it. They balance a flat lid on the stones over the coals. When it's hot, they put a drop of batter on and gently smooth it all around with the spoon like the French make crêpes. You cover it and cook it for about three or four minutes.

Uncle Ahmed called his daughter, Asha. 'Bring *Afdokle* about ten of those pancakes and some tea. You can't eat *angella* without the tea. She is starving. Look at her! I thought they had plenty of food in America.'

'Uncle, I can't eat ten pancakes. Four will be plenty for me.'

Asha brought some spiced tea with goat's milk and the *angella* on a dented tin plate. I put a little tea on the *angella* to soften it. We don't use forks or spoons, food is carefully taken with the fingers.

I had not tasted this special sour flavor for many years and I was so excited that I didn't think when I picked up the first bite.

My uncle jerked up like an angry camel when I reached for those pancakes. 'No! Stop, stop,' he shouted. 'That's your left hand, my child, it's your left hand. That is not for the food.'

I said, 'Oh Uncle, I am so sorry. I forgot. Excuse me.' I was ashamed and embarrassed. I am left-handed and I took the food with my left hand because it doesn't make much difference in the West. However, it's very important in Somalia that you don't get confused about which hand goes where. The right hand is for everything but touching your genitalia. After you go to the toilet you use your left hand to wash yourself with water. We don't have toilet paper. Only the left is for washing your genitals. The right hand is for eating, throwing, cutting, touching others and everything else.

Uncle shook his white head at me. 'Have you been gone that long? Have you forgotten what you knew?' He looked at me, 'How dare you forget to be clean. You can forget anything else in Somalia but not that.'

I was so hungry I didn't think of anything but putting food in my mouth as fast as possible. I was acting like I was in New York. I forgot about how Somalis feel about food. We don't have 'fast food'. We don't even have a concept of eating food while you are doing something else. I was taught that food is a gift from Allah. It is a blessing and must be treated with respect. You don't eat something because it tastes good, you eat to fill your belly – to keep from dying. You don't grab food and shove it in your mouth without thinking about it. You sit down, you say a little prayer of gratitude and you taste every bite. So there I was not only grabbing the food without a prayer or proper respect, but taking it with my left hand.

I took a deep breath and started over; I said thank you to Allah for my uncle, for this day and for this food. I ate the *angella* slowly and carefully. It was delicious. As I ate I watched my uncle. He had a wisp of a mustache and a few white hairs left on his chin. He was wearing a gray and black plaid *maa-a-weiss*. I started looking closely and I noticed that he was leaning against the house in a strange way. His mouth drooped and he talked very slowly like it was hard to make the words. Mohammed kept saying, '*Hiiyea*?' asking Uncle to repeat what he said.

'What happened to your father?' I asked Asha when she brought us some tea. 'Why is he leaning like that?'

'He went to sleep one night and when he woke up he could not use his left arm or leg. The one side was fine, the other was just hanging there.'

'Oh my God!' I said, 'what did the doctor tell you about it?'

'We don't have a doctor here.'

'Did you take him to the hospital?'

'No. It's too far and he couldn't walk. Why would we take him so far away when he was sick?'

'What!' I couldn't believe it. The man wakes up half paralyzed and they don't take him to the hospital. 'When did this happen?'

'A few days ago,' Asha said. 'He is better today, *Alhamdillah*.' She didn't seem to be anything but resigned to what happened and grateful to Allah that he seemed a little better. I understand why my family believes that there is a day when it is your time to die, that is the will of Allah and we have to accept death as part of life. I understand that, but at the same time they don't know that when you are sick you can be cured. They don't believe in doctors or surgeons. I can appreciate the way they feel but I think it's because they have not realized that there are other things they can do.

'Uncle,' I said, 'tell me what happened.'

'I woke up and I couldn't move my left side.' He looked patient and resigned. 'It doesn't hurt, but I can't use my left hand or raise my arm. My leg drags when I walk.'

'*Hiiyea.*'

'Your mother gave me some tea she brewed from the powdered shell of an ostrich egg and cinchona bark.'

Even though I knew that my mother's medicine cured many things I still wanted to know what was going on with my uncle. I looked at Ragge and said, 'We are taking him with us when we go to the hospital to find my father.'

Ragge shrugged and said, 'What for? How are they going to help him?'

'Well at least I want to know what happened and get him some medicine or an operation if that is what he needs,' I told him.

Asha helped her father to wash. She brought a small bowl filled with water and washed his face and arms with a little cloth. She helped him to put on a blue shirt and a jean jacket. She lifted the useless arm and fitted it into the sleeve. A relative of Asha's husband had a taxi-car and I asked if he would take us to the hospital in Galkayo. Asha helped her father to get into the back seat of the car with me, Mohammed and Ragge sat in the front. We had to drive for over three hours to get to Galkayo, but I didn't care about getting right back in another car, after our long journey the day before. There was a hospital where I hoped to find my father and a dispensary and doctors who might be able to help my uncle in Galkayo.

Sand in the Somali desert isn't like on a beach, it's dark red earth. White rocks and low-growing thorn bushes are all over, like spots on a leopard. Very quickly after it rains the desert plants start to push up out of the ground. Tiny leaves fringe the bushes and the acacia trees. Driving around that day I was surprised at how lovely it was. All of the terrible heat had evaporated with the rainstorm. The earth was a muted red, almost the color of blood, the air was so fresh and clean it felt good taking it into my lungs. Why don't the newspapers ever talk about this? It seems all they care about is chasing after trouble. Even though my poor little country has a lot of sadness, at the same time it is still beautiful. If only tears were rain.

Along the road we came to a checkpoint guarded by men who had big long guns slung over their shoulders. Ragge said there are always security forces when you cross the borders into a territory controlled by another clan.

'Hey,' I asked him in a whisper from the back seat, 'they don't use those guns do they?'

'You bet they will. They will look at what you are carrying or who is with you – believe me anything can go wrong. Maybe they just don't like you. If you are a different clan and they want money or something you better give them what they want. That's all they have to live on, it's not like they get paid or anything by the army.'

'I pray to God they don't bother us,' I said, my heart pounding. We stopped and one of the soldiers peered inside the car. We paid the toll and he opened the gate and waved us through and the other soldiers just ignored us.

When we were children we would tremble when we heard

the word, *Aba*, father. Just thinking about my father made me anxious. I had so many feelings about that man, and still I wanted to see him badly. I wanted to look my father in the face; I wanted him to look at me and see what had become of that little girl he used to order around. I wanted him to look at my face – a face that had been on magazine covers and in movies, a face that people recognized all over the world. I wanted him to remember what he said to me. 'You are not one of my children; I don't know where you came from.' That is what hurt me the most – maybe it's why I never came back all these years.

I don't know what I expected to find in the hospital in Galkayo, but my heart sank when I saw it. Most of the buildings were just walls halfway up and only a little dispensary was open. It looked like they had started working then quit before it was anywhere near being finished. There weren't piles of bricks or materials around to complete the buildings anywhere that I could see. Mohammed and Ragge helped my uncle to step out of the car and walk into the dispensary. He put one foot out and dragged the other to meet it leaning on his son and his nephew.

I looked around the place while we waited for the doctor. Only two little rooms were finished. One room had some equipment, a microscope and a few bottles of medicine. There were no cabinets of instruments or medicine or any supplies. Wooden shutters on the windows let in light and you could see just a few empty trays and bottles scattered here and there. The walls were painted with thin paint, light blue on the bottom and pink on the top. There was an eye chart on the wall in a wooden frame. The bathroom had stacks of tiles and a toilet that was not hooked up. This was it, the only medical facility for hours in any direction. What do the doctors do, how can they help people who are sick or hurt? It didn't look like they could take an X-ray or even give someone blood.

Finally a nurse came and said that my father was there and she would show us to the room where he was. Suddenly I felt very weak and scared. I had high hopes that I would see the king that I used to know but at the same time I was worried about what he'd become. I took a long deep breath and dragged slowly behind the boys.

The room was filled with people, all relatives of my father. They recognized Mohammed immediately and shouted and greeted him with hugs and shouts of joy. He turned around and said, 'This is my sister Waris,' and everybody started to call out to me but I couldn't breathe and I didn't want to see anyone but my father.

'Mohammed,' I asked him, 'don't say anything because I want to be the one who says hello to *Aba*.' I slipped between the people and went over to see my father.

He was lying on a narrow bed with two people sitting next to him. He was just lying there dozing with his eyes bandaged and his arms crossed over his body as if he was dead. I broke down. My tears came in a gush and I just sat and held his hand while they rolled down my cheeks. I didn't want anyone to see me cry or hear any sobs. I took a minute and then put my cheek next to his. He looked terrible but I thanked Allah that he was still alive and that I had found this man. I was angry with myself because I hadn't been there for so long, and so hadn't helped my family through their troubles. His hair was totally gray and he had only a small tuft of a beard. He was so thin that his cheeks sunk into his teeth. He looked fragile and broken, bewildered and lost.

Aba woke and said, 'Who is this?'

I kissed him and whispered, 'It's me Papa, Waris.'

'Who's that?' he said.

I said, 'Father, Father, it's Waris.'

'Waris?' he said slowly, 'I used to have a daughter named Waris but I don't any more – we don't know what happened to her. Please stop teasing me about that.'

'Papa, oh Papa! Really it's me.'

'What, Waris? She's been gone too long to suddenly arrive out of nowhere.'

'Father, it is me.'

'What? Is this really Waris? Oh, my daughter, my daughter. I thought you were dead and gone,' he said, turning his head towards me and squeezing my hand tightly. 'What happened to your eye?' I said, afraid to hear what he had to tell me.

'Oh, I'm all right, I'm all right. *Alhamdillah*, I am fine. Two days ago my eye was operated on.'

'Where did you have this operation? Did you go to a hospital?' I asked.

'It was done in the bush,' he said.

I couldn't believe it. 'What did they do to your eye?'

'He sliced it with his knife and took off the skin that was covering the eye.'

'Was he a doctor?' I asked. I was wondering who would slice open a person's eye outside of a hospital.

My father mumbled, 'He said he was a doctor.'

I patted his hand, 'Papa, did you have anything for the pain?'

'Child,' he said. 'What do you think? Of course I felt the pain. I could only see shadows with one eye and I am blind in the other. I felt him slicing me and I just had to lie there.'

'That is ridiculous,' I groaned out loud. 'To let somebody you don't know slice up your eye with a knife.'

'Waris! Waris, it is you – my daughter!' Father said really recognizing me. 'You haven't changed a bit. You always were a rebel and you are still making trouble.' After he said that, it brought back the way he used to be, strong and tough, a real warrior. I couldn't stop crying. 'Child, you cry when I'm dead,' he said, squeezing my hands. 'Right now I'm alive and looking for another big wife.'

That was my papa – that was the man I remembered. He joked even when he was blind and lying on a bed helpless. I looked at him for a long time, this old man who was my father. To me he was still handsome even though his age and difficult life had changed him. His face is a perfect oval and the strong creases running down either side accentuate the shape.

My father has been a nomad all his life. He has traveled from tribal wells to grasslands but never out of the Horn of Africa, never to a city with traffic or telephones. He had no way of knowing about modern medicine. He did what his family has done forever, he went to a bush doctor to cure his eyesight with a knife and a prayer to Allah. He was not angry about what happened, he accepted it and would accept whatever came next without tears and remorse. I suppose doctors and operations can't give you acceptance or peace in your heart.

I heard a voice next to me and there was my brother Burhaan. He has such a beautiful face that if he had been a girl my father would have been a happy man. He is so perfect that tribes would fight to offer the biggest bride price. He has a baby face with skin so smooth it looked like a painting. I reached up and touched him to feel the perfection and hugged him tightly. He was not quite as tall as Mohammed and he had evenly spaced features and was a perfect combination of my mother and father.

Burhaan explained that when he found *Aba* he was in bad shape due to the pain and swelling. The veins in his whole head were swollen and he was crazy with fever. Burhaan was afraid that he would die or wander off into the bush and be killed by the hyenas who waited for people like that. He brought him to the hospital and our relatives stayed with him and cared for him. In Somalia the family never leave a family member with strangers in a hospital, they camp right outside so they can say prayers and cook special foods.

I said, 'We want to take you back home with us, Papa. We have to get you home where we can take care of you. We have a car and you are in no condition to walk.'

'Home, which home?' *Aba* asked.

I said, 'You come and stay with Mohammed and me at mother's house.'

'No, I am not going to that woman's house,' he said.

'Papa,' I said, 'we have to take you with us so we can take care of you. Mohammed and I will only be here for a few more days. We love you, we want to look after you, we want you to be with us for the next ten days.'

'No,' he insisted. 'I don't want to go there. You visit me at my house.'

Burhaan reminded him that there was nobody to take care of him there and Mohammed pleaded with him until he finally agreed. We asked the doctor to release him and arranged to pick him up later that afternoon on our way back.

I then asked if a doctor could take a look at my uncle. The nurse asked us to bring him to the nearby dispensary. She wore a white lab coat and a headscarf of yellow the color of saffron rice, which covered her head and shoulders down to her waist. To me it seemed strange that a professional woman still covered her face at work. She showed us in to see the dispensary doctor and stood behind him in case he needed anything. The doctor took a blood sample from Uncle's arm. Uncle didn't even flinch when they punctured his arm with the needle. That would show weakness. He appeared calm and patient but I noticed that the veins on the side of his head stood out. The doctor looked in his eyes, took his blood pressure and tapped on his knee with a little silver hammer. He listened to his heart and looked in his ears. All that time Uncle looked at me, not the doctor. As long as I agreed with what was going on he would not say anything.

The doctor had a round face pock-marked with large moles on both cheeks. He had glasses on a chain around his neck and an enormous gold watch. It was a little too big for his wrist and moved when he gestured. He was calm and careful with everything he told me. He spoke excellent English and I felt more confident talking with him in English than in Somali. I didn't have the words to discuss modern medicine in Somali.

'What's wrong with my uncle?' I asked. 'Can you fix him?'

'We can give him some medical treatment,' he said.

'When will he be better?'

'He has hypertension and has suffered a hemorrhage in his brain.'

'Oh my God!' I said. I really didn't understand exactly what he meant but it sounded serious.

'He had a little stroke. It has caused the paralysis on his left side.' He asked my uncle to lift up his left arm. He could raise it to about shoulder height but it was a clumsy effort.

'Allah is curing you!' I said to encourage him.

'As the swelling in the brain goes down he should recover more,' the doctor said. He wrote out a prescription on a piece of paper and gave us a round bottle of pills. 'He needs to take this medicine every single day,' he told me, with an emphasis on the every. There were directions on the bottle and a flimsy paper inside. I think it was German or French but nobody back at the camp would be able to read that complicated paper.

'What will happen when the pills run out?' I asked. We had traveled for hours to get to Galkayo and I knew there were no pharmacies where my family was living, and no reliable way to get things delivered to them. You could give someone money to bring things but many times they took most of the money – or they would bring you the wrong thing.

'There are several pharmacies here in Galkayo,' the doctor told me. 'They have medicine from Europe.'

I hoped that Uncle would be better after taking the pills in the bottle because I didn't trust that he would get more. 'Is there anything he shouldn't eat?' Diet might be something he could control. 'How about sugar?' I felt like I had to push this man to tell me anything – he didn't explain things. I wanted to know how this happened, how someone can just wake up paralyzed, but he carefully picked every single word he said.

'No sugar, no salt. Anything else he can eat.'

'How long have you been here?' I inquired. Behind him a hand-written sign was taped on the wall. It said, Dr Ahmed Abdillahi. I wondered how much he knew about what nomadic people eat – as much milk and animal fat as they can get, because vegetables and fruits are not available most of the time.

'Here in Puntland?' he asked. He didn't say Somalia – or even Somaliland.

'Yes, here in Puntland.'

'I received my degree in Italy in 1970,' he replied. 'I am a neurosurgeon.'

I had to be honest with the man. I said, 'How can you help people with what you've got here, which is nothing.'

'This will be one of the finest hospitals in the Horn of Africa,' he said earnestly. 'We are constructing a new hospital with aid from the UK. When the hospital is fully open we will be able to do surgery.'

'What is the major medical problem you deal with?' I asked.

'I really can't say,' he told me.

'Is it AIDS?'

'We do see that but not too much.'

'Why can't you tell me what the major medical problem is?'

'I am a surgeon. You will have to ask someone else that question.'

I tried to find out more from some of the other people around the hospital, but nobody wanted to talk to me. I asked one doctor wearing a face-mask how long he had been here.

'Only one month,' he said.

'What is the major medical problem you have encountered so far?'

'TB,' he said and turned back to his Bunsen burner.

We decided to shop since we were in Galkayo. I had not been able to stop thinking about food since we arrived, since there wasn't much around. Getting food, eating food, having food around was suddenly very important. I forgot what it is like not to have cupboards full of pasta and flour and sugar, or a refrigerator with milk and eggs and bread. I looked for a corner store stocked with bread and cheese and canned things, but we didn't pass any. There is no refrigeration and everything has to be eaten the day you get it. Even if you had money there didn't seem to be much food around. The little stores were basically empty. Mohammed asked someone to direct us to the *suq* or market. 'Oh, that's all closed now. Everybody has gone away,' the man said. He was tall and had to lean over to look in the window, which he did for a long time. 'Who is that?' he asked Mohammed, offended because I didn't have my head covered. Though it was hot in that headscarf, I was embarrassed and pulled it up over my head until he left. Why did I respond to some old nomad I'll never see again? Because in my bones I'm a Somali woman.

We stopped in front of a little shop with an open door and empty metal barrels scattered around the front. A sleepy man in a turban got up and stood behind the counter when we came in. He had a few bolts of cloth on the shelves behind him, a box of batteries and some plastic shoes. He looked like he didn't trust strangers. Mohammed and I had changed a hundred dollars into Somali shillings in Abu Dhabi. They gave me 2,620 shillings in battered, ripped and dirty money for every dollar. The money had a picture of Siad Barre on it and I suppose it was the last official currency printed by the government. The shopkeeper wouldn't accept the shillings. 'That kind of money is for the other parts of Somalia,' he said and handed it back to Mohammed. 'We use the money from Puntland. It has a picture of Mohammed Egal, the head of the government of Puntland,' he said firmly.

'How can you have some people who only accept one kind of money, and others who won't let you buy anything if you have that kind of money?' I asked Mohammed when he sat back down in the car.

'That's the way things are here.' We found a woman willing to sell some green oranges, and some packets of tea and spices wrapped in newspapers tightly folded into squares. We bought rice in newspaper wrapped like a cone.

Late that afternoon everybody was tired and hungry so we stopped to eat in a little place that looked like a garage. Even though it was late in the day they still had lamb, goat meat, rice, and pasta. You could order tea, melon or papaya juice, or water. I was hungry and I had a delicious meal. I had a nice long glass of melon juice and lots of pasta. I didn't eat the meat because I am very suspicious of meat unless I cook it myself. The cook put a slice of meat on my tin plate but it was tough. One thing I didn't understand was why they didn't cook the meat well enough. When they cook it in a sauce it is tender and falls apart. I stuck to pasta and sauce. I was worried about getting sick and asked, 'Do you have any bottled water?' They even had bottles of Somali spring water! The waiter brought me a bottle of *Ali Mohammed Jama* spring water. 'Mohammed, we should do something like this, we should build a factory,' I told him. Mohammed wasn't interested and we ate quickly in order to get back to pick up my father and Burhaan at the hospital.

My brother, Mohammed, was in control of the money, or so he thought, so he paid the bill. I kept the dollars and he kept the Somali money. It was confusing because of the two presidents on the different kinds of money, one was from the Hawiye, the other was printed by the Daarood in the South. Each kind was worth a different amount. I had to keep asking, 'How much is this? How much is that?'

Mohammed usually replied, 'Never mind, I'll take care of it.' He knew what was what and I didn't want to be taken advantage of, so that was fine with me. My uncle was hot and tired so we stopped at a cousin's house to visit. He needed to rest for a while before we tried to go all the way back to the village over those rough roads. While we were in Galkayo, and Uncle was resting, I wanted to change some money at a bank.

I told Mohammed, 'I don't want you coming with me. You give me too much trouble.'

Mohammed started to argue with me as soon as I said it. My brother's eyes were flashing. 'I should come with you Waris, you don't know what you are doing.'

'Don't worry about it, Mohammed. Ragge and me will go. You stay here with Uncle.' Mohammed flipped out and walked away in a huff. When I tried to get him to tell me what was the matter he told me not to trust Ragge.

'He may be family but he is not as close as your brother,' he said. 'Don't give him the money to change at the bank, you don't know how much you will get in exchange.'

My brother and I are too much alike. I had had enough of him telling me what to do all the time. I walked out of the house with Ragge and we drove over to the bank.

Women don't go into a bank in Muslim countries so I waited outside. I gave Ragge about four hundred and fifty dollars and I sat in the car in front of the bank while he went in to change the money. The bank looked like a storage building, it was a big box with a door. Ragge came right back and gave me everything I asked for arranged in three stacks. I changed a hundred dollars for my father, two hundred and fifty to give to my mother, and one hundred dollars for our trip. Ragge gave me every shilling and he wrote the names on the different stacks. The money was a mixture of both currencies so we were prepared for people who would only accept one or the other.

When we got back to our cousin's house Mohammed was so angry he wouldn't talk to me for the first hour. He looked the other way and ignored me he was so mad. It didn't matter because people started to fill up the room. They had heard that we were visiting and came to say hello. I have a very big family, even relations I never heard of, never imagined, never dreamt about. Everybody wanted to meet me, to say hello. It felt wonderful and terrible at the same time. I loved being a part of such a big family, and meeting so many people who cared about me. However, many of the relatives I met needed or wanted something from me and that was hard. What could I do for them? My uncle Ali called to a little girl and told her to come and sit down next to me.

'This little child is very ill. She needs you to help her,' he said.

'What is the matter with her?' I asked taking her little hand in mine.

'She has a disease.'

'Do you know what the name of the disease is?'

'No, but all of her hair has fallen out and she is wasting away. She is a feather and does not grow.'

I couldn't see her to find out what was wrong because she was wearing a long dress and had a headscarf wrapped all around her head and face like most Somali girls.

'I want you to take her back to the United States and take care of her there.'

'Uncle,' I said, 'I would like to help you but I really can't.'

'Why won't you help this child?' he said. 'I know that if you take her she can get better. Here she cannot be cured – we have no medicine for this sickness. You have to take this child and look after her and save her,' he begged me.

'Please Uncle, I have so many problems and responsibilities of my own that you don't know about. Just because I live in the West doesn't mean that I live in luxury.'

'What problems could you have?' he said. 'Here we have fighting and crazy soldiers with guns. We don't have a proper hospital or enough food all the time. What kind of problems can be worse than that?'

There was no way he could understand that it would be impossible for me to take a sick child back to New York with me. I knew that I could not accept the responsibility for her. 'Uncle, I will pray for her but I can't take her back with me. You must try to understand.' I stroked her hand and hugged her then I got up and said that we really had to go and pick up my father. It was getting late.

When we left I sat in the back with my uncle. Mohammed was still angry and he would not even look at me. He sat in the front and stared at the road. We went right back to the hospital to pick up my father and Burhaan but it was dark by the time we left Galkayo and you couldn't see much of anything. It must have been over one hundred miles back to my mother's village. A little way out of town my father asked where we were going and when I explained, he said he had changed his mind and didn't want to come back with us to my mother's place.

'No, I am not going there,' he insisted, a helpless old man with his face covered in bandages and too weak to walk. My uncle tried to talk to him. He and my father were sitting next to each other and my uncle put his arms around his brother and talked to him softly, calmly. It was the first time I ever saw them hold each other, two old men, two brothers. It was a beautiful moment in the middle of such sadness for both of them. How time had bent them.

My father would not relent however, and I begged him to come and stay with us for a few days. 'I have not seen you for twenty years,' I said. 'Mohammed and I will only be here for a few days and if you don't stay with us I will not get to see you. Please come with us.' He finally agreed to stay with us but he wanted to go back to his little mud-brick house and get some things first.

'Father,' I asked, 'where is your place?'

'Just go that way,' he answered waving his left hand in the air.

I tried again. 'Father, it's pitch black outside and we can't see anything.'

He got very short and insisted in a loud voice, 'Just go where I tell you, child! I know what I am doing, just go where I tell you.' My brothers and I had to laugh at this old man sitting in the back seat who can't see or drive and was still insisting that the driver go where he says. Even Mohammed had to give up his anger and see the irony in the situation. Blind and helpless, my father still ruled the roost. The only lights were the car headlights and they showed nothing but rocks and dust. My father pointed to the left and so we turned off the road and traveled right into the rolling desert. All at once my father said, 'Turn here, turn here,' but there was a lot of nothing. 'Is there a termite mound over there? Can you see the *dadune*?' he said.

'Yes, I see them,' Mohammed said, surprised.

'Well you have to turn left,' Father said, as if he had driven this route every night of his life. I had no idea what he was doing – we could not see more than six feet in front of the car and we were driving with no road, no track, nothing but my father's blind directions.

After about fifteen minutes my father said, 'Can you see it?'

'See what, Father?' Mohammed asked.

'My house,' he announced with total assurance. 'My house is right over there.' Sure enough the car lights showed a couple of huts over a little hill. 'OK we're here,' he said calmly.

I said, 'Which one is it? Where is your house?'

My father made a face and said, 'I think it's the one with a red door.' Then he reconsidered, 'Was it red?'

I said, 'Father, we have no idea which one is your house.'

He said, 'Well, I think the door is red. Take the torch and look for red.' We had no idea what else to do so we just went over to the first house. Mohammed opened the door and shone the light inside on a poor woman with three kids. We said, 'Oh excuse us. Sorry.' We shone the torch on the second house. Sure enough, it had a red door. It was empty – nothing inside but a dirt floor.

I went back out to him in the car. 'I think we've found it, but what are we looking for Father?'

'My shirts.' I asked him where they would be and he said, 'I don't know child. They will be in there – sitting in the corner.' I bent over and crawled into the tiny house and felt around on the packed earth floor. Sure enough, there were two shirts and an army jacket. They were filthy lying there in the dirt. There were stains all over them from the sand and his sweat had left half-moon white shapes under the arms. The smell was terrible. I left them right there and told him, 'Father, you don't need those things, they are dirty.'

'Bring them,' he snapped at me. There were no locks on the door so we just closed it and went back to the car. As we were about to get in I noticed three little kids standing next to the car talking to my father. I asked him who they were and he replied, 'Say hello, these are your brothers.' He explained that the mother of these children was a woman he divorced last week. I asked them to come in front of the car, in the light, so I could see them. They were skinny things with trusting eyes all under ten years old. I had only a little moment in the car lights to see my half-brothers before we had to entrust them to Allah and the peaceful desert. My father didn't offer any explanation and I knew better than to ask. I hoped I could find out about them

from my mother when we got back. But how my blind old
father led us back to his house in the dark – that I shall
never understand.

On the long journey home I sat between him and my
uncle, holding on to both of them. I felt so blessed. I had my
father and my uncle and my brothers and I was home in my
beautiful country. Yes, I was tired and worn out, but I didn't
care, other things were so much more important. I couldn't
stop myself from thinking about all the differences between
my life in New York, where food and comfort is everywhere,
and the life my family leads, here in Somalia. Most people in
the West have so many things they don't even know what
they have. My parents could probably count every single
thing they owned, and food was difficult to get, yet they
were cheerful and happy. People on the street were smiling
and talking to each other. I think that Western people are
trying to fill themselves up with something that is missing.
Everybody there is searching. They search in the stores and
on the television. People have shown me a room in their
house where they have candles for prayer and meditation. A
whole room just for the candles. Here we all had to squeeze
together so there was enough space on the sleeping mat for
everyone. It was not a problem, it was joy to be all together;
everyone kept saying thank you Allah that we are all
together. In Somalia we don't have a special place for prayer,
we pray even when we greet someone. 'May Allah be with
you,' we say. In New York everyone says 'hello'. What does
that mean? Hello. It doesn't mean anything that I know of,
it's just something that you say. People say 'have a good day',
but it's just something that you say. 'If God is willing, I'll see
you later,' we say in Somali. God had been willing and my
first day with my family was a good day, a very good day!

9

tribal talk

A woman's beauty is not in her face

Somali Proverb

When we finally arrived back in the village my mother was sitting near the fire petting her goats and telling stories to Nhur, her granddaughter, and Mohammed *Inyer*. When she saw my brothers guiding my father between them she said to me, 'Allah! You brought him with you? How is he?'

'Go and ask him yourself,' I said to her. She went over to them and said, 'Well, well, what have we here? Did you find a stray camel in the bush?' Then she gently touched my father's bandage and said, 'How are you doing in there?' with her wicked sense of humor. She asked me to go with her to get some cloths to make him a bed.

'I'm surprised that your father agreed to come back here,' my mother said when we were alone.

'Why? Is it because he didn't want you to see him like this?'

'No! Waris, Burhaan never paid the bride price for Nhur,' she whispered in my ear. 'Your father kept saying he would pay it when he got the money. She has been married to Burhaan for two years and she's on her second child. Her father and brothers have been complaining about it.'

'Oh. She is such a sweet person, I love her already.'

'She takes good care of me and Burhaan. Her father is worried about what would happen if Burhaan kicks her out – she was a clean new bride. Now they are demanding the money for her. Your father promised Burhaan that he would give him some camels for her but instead of doing that he went and told a cousin that she wasn't worth five camels. He said that she was lazy and didn't work and so he would not pay.'

'No! Nhur is the first one up in the morning – she works harder than everyone. That woman is a queen,' I said.

'Well, it got back to her family and they said they were going to find your father and beat him. Nhur heard what he said about her and now he is ashamed to face her.' My mother sighed. Maybe my father couldn't bear to part with the few camels he had left, but that was no excuse for not paying the bride price he promised to Nhur's family.

In Somalia, on their wedding night, brides are cut open to allow their husbands entry. A woman takes a knife and slices through her circumcision to make an opening big enough for intercourse. Her mother-in-law inspects her daughter-in-law in the morning to see if she is bleeding and has slept with her husband despite the pain. If the blood between her legs is fresh the women will dance through the village and announce it to everyone. Everyone in the village had heard my mother singing about Nhur's bravery and that she was a clean virgin when she married Burhaan. They knew how hard she worked. They knew that she had to be cut open in order to give birth to her daughter, then sewn shut again. It was obvious that my father just didn't want to pay the bride price. Everyone was calling him a coward and cheap. 'He has to go and tell them that his camels were stolen and he doesn't have the money,' I said. 'Not go around saying that she wasn't worth it.'

We went back out with our arms full of cushions just in time to see Nhur greet her husband. Although they would never kiss in public the look on her face showed how much she loved my brother. Nhur walked directly over to where my father was standing with Mohammed. She said, 'Welcome *Aba*, Father,' keeping her eyes on the ground in respect even though he could not see. He shrank back a little bit when he recognized her voice and she reached out to him and gently took his hands and reassured him, '*Aba*, you must be tired. Come with me, we have a nice bed for you.' What a beautiful woman my brother married. We are all lucky to have such dignity and grace in our family. My mother arranged most of the little cloths and pillows she owned outside her little house for my father. Nhur helped him tenderly and slowly to lie down. He was tired but would not show it until he collapsed into the pillows.

My brothers slept with my father like they had when I was a child. The women slept in the *occle* with the little children and the men and boys stayed outside to guard the animals.

The next morning when I got up it felt like a dream. I had ached for that morning – waking up with my whole family. All that was missing were my sisters and Aleeke. The men were all still sleeping and I laughed when I saw three pairs of long legs sticking out from underneath the sheets. They were all intertwined with each other and you couldn't tell whose legs were whose. It had rained during the night and since there was nowhere to go they tried to cover themselves with a sheet of plastic, but the edges of the sheets were soaked and muddy. My mother had already been out to gather firewood and Nhur had been to the market to get breakfast ready for everybody before they woke up. She left before the first light to make sure and get the best things that were available. She was making *angella* and the smell drove me crazy. When Mother came back from chasing her goats she had milk for the tea in her tin cup with a blue rim. She looked at the tangle of legs and remarked, 'Are those men going to sleep all day?' My mother never whispers – you can hear her voice everywhere. That got everybody up.

The first thing I did that morning was find my father's filthy shirts and wash them in a flat pan. You use a good scrub to clean things because we don't use a lot of water since it has to be carried a long way back to the camp. I got as much dirt out of the shirts as I could, then I wrung them a little and spread them out on thorn bushes to dry in the sun. My father was lying on his cloth near the house and he heard me. He called out, 'Who's there?'

I said, 'It's just me Father, Waris.'

He said, 'Come over here, Waris, I need to talk to you.' My father told me that he wanted to discuss the fight I had with Mohammed over Ragge and the money. I remembered that nothing passes by my father without him knowing about it. Even if you whisper right up next to someone's ear, he will hear it. He said, 'Last night I heard you and Mohammed arguing about Ragge.' My father told me not to trust Ragge with anything, especially money.

I said, 'Why not? Ragge is your own brother's son. Mohammed and Ragge were raised like brothers! Isn't my brother's brother, my brother too?'

He said, 'Yes, but you don't know anything about him, Waris. You just got here. He is showing you this face now, but you don't know him. Listen to me, I don't want you to have anything to do with him.'

'I don't understand why you are so against him,' I told him. Ragge spoke good English and I could really talk to him. He understood me and I could say things to him that Mohammed and Burhaan did not understand. Sometimes I didn't think my brothers wanted to understand me, it seemed like they were really trying to control me. I have lived on my own too long to back down when a man says this or that.

My father propped himself up with one hand and I could see that it was painful for him to move. 'Listen to me Waris: your blood brothers and you against your half-brothers. Your brothers and half-brothers and you against your cousins. Your clan against other clans. Your tribe against another tribe.'

'*Aba*, I don't believe all this clan and tribal stuff.' I sat down and took his hand. 'What is the problem with Ragge? What has he done to make you feel that he can't be trusted?'

'Ragge is a terrible son and he doesn't treat his father right,' my father insisted. 'He should be taking care of his father and the family herds. He is a conniver, you only just got here – you won't see that side of him.'

Mohammed and Burhaan returned and overheard what we were talking about. They both sided with my father and started lecturing me. 'You stupid blind girl. Listen to what *Aba* is telling you. Why are you arguing with him?'

'Don't call me that,' I said, and told the three of them to stop pushing me around to get me to believe in something I didn't. I knew what they were saying – that your own blood family is the most trustworthy, but I don't think that is always true. Just because someone is not a blood sibling doesn't mean they will take advantage of you. I couldn't understand what they were talking about, or why it was so important to spend all morning discussing it so intently, but that is how we are. Talk, discussion, argument, is the breath of life in Somali families.

Mama came around the corner and she had a funny look on her face and I knew something was up.

'Why are you smiling like that, Mama?' I said. She looked away like she had a big secret; her eyes were shining in the morning sun. I looked up and a man almost as tall as Mohammed came around the corner of the house. He stopped and started looking hard at me. I was staring at him too. My mother was cackling at the two of us.

'Don't you recognize your little baby brother?' she said.

This man had a very familiar posture and look about him but I could not place him. He squinted at me in the sun, and stuck out his tongue. It was my baby brother, Rashid, all grown up. He was a handsome man with a little mustache and a short beard under his chin. He had grown tall and straight with long arms and legs and a smile that showed off two rows of perfectly white square teeth. He was wearing a green *goa* with a bright gold pattern draped over his shoulders and a brown checked shirt. Rashid had been out in the bush herding my father's camels, or what was left of the herd, and had just come back from the desert to see if he could get some supplies. He didn't know that Mohammed and I were coming, but now here he was. What a miracle! No wonder my mother was smiling. I couldn't remember one time during my whole childhood when we were all together, my brothers and I. One or another would be off somewhere. Mohammed lived in the city, somebody was off looking for food or water or taking care of the camels in the bush. I ran away when my little brother Rashid was still a baby boy running around without pants.

I hugged him tightly and felt his strong bones in my embrace. He and Mohammed started hugging and kidding around. 'Let me get my camera, I want to take a picture of my beautiful brothers,' I said and went inside the hut and rummaged through my bags to find it. When I got back outside, both those boys had disappeared. My mother had gone to give the orange rinds and the *angella* she didn't eat from breakfast to her little goats. I started looking around for my brothers.

In the back of the house, a little distance from the village was a big termite mound. It looked like a giant brown thumb poking up out of the ground at an angle. Rashid was sitting on the top. I remembered climbing up on those things as a girl. My mother told me that the tiny termites build the enormous mounds from their own saliva. That is a tribe who works together she taught me. 'I used to climb ones five times as big,' I called. Rashid made faces at me and stuck out his long tongue again. I wished I could climb up there too but I was not wearing pants, I had on a long Somali dress and was finding it impossible to do anything with it. 'I wish I could take this damn blanket off and climb up there like I used to,' I said to him. As a child I used to grab hold of the back hem of the dress and pull it up to the front where I could tuck it into the waist and make a kind of pant. I was tempted to try it, but I finally decided I was too old for that and I didn't want to offend anyone.

I looked at Rashid climbing on the termite mound, and noticed that he had bare feet. Here he was, a grown man, and he didn't have a pair of shoes. My own brother didn't own a single pair. The bottoms of his feet were so calloused and cracked they looked like elephant hide. The one thing that I could not get over was how rough the ground was. It's covered with sharp jagged edged rocks, and I remembered how those rocks cut and hurt my feet. I didn't have shoes as a child, and here I was looking at my brother, twenty years old and still going around without shoes. I decided that he was having nice sturdy leather sandals no matter what. I would find them in a shop, or get a *midgann* to make them for him, but my brother was not going to walk back into the desert barefoot. I said, 'Rashid I'm going to make sure that you've got a pair of shoes to walk back.'

'Why don't you give me the money for the shoes?' he said. 'I'll buy my own.'

I was worried that he wanted the money to buy *khat* so I said, 'Let's go over to the market and you can pick out the ones you want.'

I thanked Allah that I was able to buy some shoes for Rashid, to get medicine for my father and my uncle. We walked together back to my mother's hut. She was using her little pile of firewood to make tea and some rice and beans for our meal.

'What did they do for Uncle Ahmed in the hospital?' Rashid asked me. 'I heard there is a *djinn* in one side of his body.'

'The doctor examined him and gave him a little bottle of pills,' I told him. 'I can't tell you much more than that. The people there didn't really want to talk to me – to spend any time with me.'

'Who was the doctor?' Rashid wanted to know.

'What do you mean?' I asked. 'He said he was trained in Italy and was a neurosurgeon.'

'No, I mean who are his clansmen?'

'Well, I don't know. What does that have to do with it?'

'If we are not related he is not going to take the same

time and care of you that he would for people in his own tribe.'

'He's a doctor and they don't care what tribe you are,' I said. 'I don't think he wanted to talk to a woman. He's used to dealing with men and he probably thinks that women are stupid.'

'*Hiiyea*,' Rashid replied. He had to agree with that. He saw my mother walk by and asked her who was wearing the shoes.

Everybody was constantly fighting over one pair of flip-flops. They only had one good pair in the whole house and I kept hearing, 'Where are the shoes? I need to go to the bathroom. It's almost time to pray, I have to wash.' Mama would have them on to get something outside, and Burhaan would have to wait until she came back and gave him the shoes so he could go to the bathroom. 'Who is wearing the shoes?' I heard all day – especially just before it was time to pray and everybody had to go and wash. Four people were fighting for one pair of rubber flip-flops. They were the cheap kind that fall apart two days after you buy them. The front piece that goes between your toes comes out and they won't stay on your feet any more. My mother was wearing two different colors when I met her and half of the bottom of one was missing. I said, 'Let's go to the market and see if we can get some more shoes then you won't have to waste so much time waiting for them.'

Rashid flashed a big row of pearly teeth in my direction, 'You don't own time, Waris. How can you waste it?'

I could see that he was a tease. 'Well, talking to you is a waste of time,' I joked. He and Ragge walked with me over to the outdoor market. Ragge wanted me to buy him a pair of black boots. I looked at him and said, 'Hey what are you going to do with boots? It's hot here, those are for London.'

My cousin's got his own unique fashion thing going on so I bought them for him. I bought two pairs of flip-flops and some incense and a mortar and pestle to grind fresh spices. Rashid didn't like any of the shoes in the market and we decided to look another day. He did like my sunglasses and I gave them to him. They would protect his eyes from the sun when he watched after my father's herds.

That night I had a big discussion about clans and tribes with my brothers and the rest of the family. My father is Daarood, the major tribe in the Central/Southern parts of Somalia. His sub-clan is Majeerteen. My family has always lived in the Haud, an area that is on the border with Ethiopia. My father's name is Dahee Dirie. My mother is from another major tribe, the Hawiye. She was raised in Mogadishu in what was once considered the capital of the whole of Somalia. When my father went to her mother and asked about marrying her he was turned down by her family. 'You are Daarood – you are a wild man – how will you support my daughter? You are not our people.' My mother ran away with him and she has never looked back. Now her brothers and sisters are all over the world. She is the only one lost in the desert.

There are four major clans in Somalia: Dir, Daarood, Isaaq and Hawiye. The majority of the Somali people belong to one of those clans and everyone is Muslim and speaks Somali. There are some smaller ones, the Rahanwayn and the Digil, but those people live mostly in the far south of the country near Kismayu. The people in our clan family were traditionally pastoral, only now more people are living in towns. As nomads move constantly the clan is more important than an address that changes all the time. This is not something that Europeans understand very well. When they decided the borders for Somalia they scattered Somalis around several different countries. The five stars on the Somali flag stand for Somalia, Somaliland, Djibouti and the Ogaden, as well as the Somalis in Kenya.

This clan business didn't seem all that important to me when I was growing up except I was proud to be a Daarood because it was the most fearless clan and I mean fearless. The nickname of the Daarood people is *Libah*, the Lion. Now I wanted to understand it. It was certainly important to my father and brothers and played a role in what was going on in my country. Siad Barre first said he was going to abolish tribalism then he started to provoke tribal conflict in an effort to distract everyone from the problems he was having. In 1991 after Siad Barre left the country and his government collapsed everybody got together with members of their clans to try to establish a base of power. These attempts to gain power left my country in a big mess. I think the whole clan thing is ridiculous and I told my brothers what I thought.

'The only thing that is destroying Somalia is tribalism,' I said.

'Daarood is the biggest and the strongest clan in this country,' said Burhaan. 'It is the major clan at this point, Waris.'

'Yes,' I replied, 'and it's also the proudest and the most fearless.' I knew that even if you are trying to save your life and you lie about being Daarood, they will know. 'Everybody should have a say in the government,' I told him.

'We should say what happens here,' he said, 'I'm not sharing power with anybody from those other clans.'

I told him, 'This clan business is keeping this country from solving problems. If you left Somalia you would see that we are all the same people! We all live in the same land, we all speak the same language, we look alike and we think

alike. We have got to get together and end this feuding.' I
was blazing mad about this now we were talking about it. To
the rest of the world we are all Somali, but here, people
could not get along with each other.

My mother brought us some tea and Rashid started to kid
around with me.

'Waris, who are you? Can you recite your lineage?' he
asked.

'I am Daarood,' I said.

'Yes, but what are you after that?'

'Well, Waris Dirie,' I said and they all started laughing. 'I
take my father's name, Dahee, then my grandfather's name,
Dirie, Mohammed, Sulimann.' They laughed at me because
it goes on for thirty names and I couldn't remember more
than the first three. I said, 'Hey, they are all dead.' My
mother's name is Fattuma Ahmed Aden and she started
reciting her father and her grandfather and her great
grandfather and on and on. The children are given the
father's names, but a woman keeps her own father's names
when she marries. My brothers started trying to teach me all
of my ancestor's names. I couldn't get it and they would
not slow down so I couldn't even hear the way they were pro-
nounced. They started reciting our lineage like rap music.
The clan rap sheets all start with a common ancestor and
you keep adding a name each generation. My family thinks
that the more names (generations) you have, the more prestigious the clan.

Finally I said, 'I'll tell you, as soon as I left Somalia I didn't
have any use for that and I never paid any more attention to
any of it. What is so important about remembering a bunch
of names?' I asked them. 'What difference has this made to
you, Mohammed, in Amsterdam? All of this hasn't fed me or
anything.'

Mohammed was quiet, like he was remembering something terrible. 'When *Afweine* first took over the government, he started a lot of different projects. He decided that Somali would be written in the Latin script and opened schools. When *Afweine* ran out of money to pay the teachers he suddenly decided that the students had to go into the bush and teach the nomads. He had a big literacy campaign.'

'I remember that,' I said. 'You tried to teach me and Old Man the letters.'

'Yes, but I was a city boy,' Mohammed said. 'I thought you were stupid nomads. I didn't want to come out to the bush and I didn't want to teach you anything.'

'I remember that too!' I said. 'You hit me with the writing stick.'

'*Afweine* turned out to be the biggest tribalist of all,' Mohammed sighed. 'If nine men wanted to meet with him he would only talk separately with members of each clan. There were a lot of murders of the Isaaq clan, just because they were Isaaq,' Mohammed muttered, and he stopped talking like he didn't want to remember it.

'Waris, your clansmen are the ones who are going to help you when you need it,' Burhaan said. 'That doctor in the hospital was not helpful because he is not one of our people.'

'He's supposed to help everybody,' I said.

'Consider how we got here in the first place,' Mohammed added. 'We got a driver to bring us because he belongs to our family. He has a reason to help us – he knows that when he needs something we are going to give it to him if we have it.'

Before that visit to Somalia in 2000 I was happy that they had a new president for the first time since 1991 and I thought that many problems could be solved. Now I saw that they still couldn't get behind one person. 'So how are you going to have a country if the clans won't work with each other?' I said.

Burhaan said, 'There are two countries.'

'Well, how does that work?'

'One is in the North, called Somaliland, and the other is Somalia in the South. Then there is Puntland in the north-east around Galkayo,' Burhaan said. 'That's why there are two different kinds of money, one is left over from Siad Barre in the South and the other is Mohammed Ibrahim Egal's money from Somaliland in the North.'

When I was a child the tribal elders solved problems. Suppose you fought with somebody and managed to knock out an eye. His clan would demand compensation for the loss of an eye from your clan. That is called *diya* – paying. Men from the two clans would meet under a big tree and they would sit there until they had figured out what the loss of an eye was worth. Of course if you knocked out a woman's eye that would be worth a lot less than a man's eye. Everybody would have to contribute and those animals would be distributed to the members of the blinded man's clan. Nowadays people would say: hey, I live in Mogadishu; I didn't have anything to do with that man hitting the other one. I am not paying for his troubles.

'We need a government based on laws not this clan business,' I said but nobody wanted to hear about it, they could not see how it would work. Mohammed insisted that the old ways were dead and gone. 'Elders are no longer respected and the so-called military leaders can't control their own troops.' My brothers went on talking so I went to sit with the women and watch the moon rise between the clouds and light up my desert home.

I saw my mother walk over to the neighbors with a cup of goat milk. She had four goats to her name in this world and here she was bringing some milk to share with the woman next door. I watched her go between the row of little huts surrounded by thorn fences carefully carrying her little tin cup with the blue rim. She had on the same dress she always wore with a little torn scarf that she wrapped around her head. She had her broken pair of mis-matched flip-flops on her feet. She stooped down and went into the neighbor's house for a few little minutes. She came out quietly and stood back up. She rested her hands on her back for a moment and looked up at the sunset colors streaking the big sky from end to end. She walked back and dangled her empty cup on her finger and hung it on the nail outside her door. That was my Mama. That is the kindness I used to know; that's a neighbor.

'Mama, sit down for a minute. I want to show you the things I brought for you,' I begged her. The woman never sat down, she was moving from morning till night. What I really wanted to give to my mother was everything that she never had in life.

She gave me one of her half smiles and a funny sigh. 'I can only imagine what you brought,' she joked. Of course she wondered what I could possibly bring her from New York City that would be of any use. Mama looked around and said, 'Not out here Waris. If anybody sees you giving things away everybody in the whole town is going to come and sit there until you give them something too.' She was right. My relatives would never ask for anything, but they would sit there and look at you until you finally broke down and offered them a present. Nhur and Mama came with me into her little house and we lit a *feynuss.*

Nhur immediately started to rummage through my bag like a vulture, asking, 'What's this? What is this for?'

'Hold on, hold on,' I said, 'I know what's what and I'm going to tell you if you just wait a minute.' I took out a jar of cocoa butter. 'That is *subaq*,' I said and opened it so she could try it. Before I could stop them, both she and my mother stuck their fingers into it and licked it.

'Ug! This is horrible, no wonder you're so skinny – if that's what they have to eat in New York.'

'Hey,' I said, 'you don't eat cocoa butter. It's for your hands and skin.'

'You can't cook with it?' my mother said.

'No, it's lotion for your face, for your dry feet – for your skin.'

'Well, it smelled so lovely why can't I eat it?'

'It's only for your skin. Don't eat it.'

'OK, OK, I won't eat it but *subaq ghee* is a lot better than that stuff. You can cook with it and use it on your skin. What else do you have?' Mama asked, handing it back to me with a shrug.

I gave her a bottle of Johnson's baby oil. 'Now what is this?' she said turning it over in her hand.

'This is oil. You can put it on your face and everywhere you want, even in your hair. It's just like the cocoa butter.'

'OK,' she said but instead of taking a drop she squeezed the bottle too hard and it squirted out all over the dirt floor. That frightened my mother and she jumped back and dropped the bottle on the sand. 'What is that stuff?' she demanded rubbing it between her fingers.

'Smell it, Mama,' I said. 'You put it on your skin or on the baby's skin.'

My mother sniffed her hand and sniffed it again. 'Oh!' she smacked her lips in approval. 'That is very beautiful. I do like that, Waris.' She rubbed it up and down her arms and they glowed in the lamplight. 'I'm going to have to hide it.'

I said, 'Mama, no. This is not a big deal. If somebody wants some of this just give it to them. I'll bring all the baby oil you want.'

'I don't know when I'm going to see you again and I'm not taking that chance,' she told me and she got up and began to search in her little pile of belongings. Deep in the bottom of a basket she found a key. She unlocked a battered wooden box and carefully tucked the baby oil inside. 'That is very precious, and it will be safe in here,' she said patting the box before she put it back in the corner.

I brought a bunch of little mirrors and a beautiful one for my mother because she never saw herself in a mirror. I wanted her to know how beautiful she is. I got my looks from my mother and they provided me with a way to support myself for a long time. Her beauty has been a great friend to me. People often tell me that I am beautiful, but if I had a drop of my mother's beauty then maybe I would believe it. I unwrapped the tissue paper from the special mirror I bought for her. It had a silver handle and leaves carved all around it that twined into beautiful flowers on the back. 'Mama,' I said, 'I brought you something very special.'

'*Hiiyea*,' she said. 'I don't need anything special, Waris.'

'Mama,' I said. 'Come and sit next to me and see what I brought for you.' When I handed it to her she looked at the wrong side in puzzlement and didn't know quite what it was. I turned it over and held it up for her. 'Look at yourself, see how beautiful you are.' When Mama finally caught her reflection she thought that someone was behind her and she jumped back in fright. I said, 'No, Mama there is nobody there. That is you.' I held the mirror up again for her. She looked at herself, she looked away, then she looked again and again. She started to touch her face and her hair with her fingers. She pulled her cheeks back, looked at her teeth and twisted her head this way and that. She studied her face for a long time and then she moaned, 'Oh, my God! Allah! I look so old. I look terrible. I didn't know I looked like this.'

'Mama!' I whispered. 'How can you say that?'

'Look at me!' she answered. Mama stared at me then she looked at Nhur; her eyes squinted in the dim light. 'What happened to my face?' she sighed. 'I used to be a beautiful woman and your father and you all sucked my life out of me.' She turned the mirror over and handed it back to me.

I didn't know what to say. I was surprised as much as hurt. My mother does not pretend about anything. She is straight out with exactly how she feels and she certainly did not pretend to like my gift. I quickly tucked it back in my bag out of sight, sorry that I had given it to her. I felt ashamed and wanted to get rid of it. She wouldn't take something that she didn't need because possessions are difficult to haul around on trek. The important things are your family, your stories, and your animals. They are the source of life and the well-spring of joy. My mother was beautiful to me because of the way she took care of her family and her friends and her animals. Real beauty is not something you see in a mirror or on the cover of a magazine; it's the way that you live your life.

10

fathers and men

The man may be the head of the house; the wife is its heart.

Somali Saying

The next day was so beautiful I felt personally blessed by
Allah. There were some high thin clouds and the morning
was a fine one. We saw some lightning at dawn, an omen of
rain. The intense heat of the previous days evaporated,
chased away by the rain. Most importantly, my family was
altogether. What a miracle! A little voice inside my head
whispered, 'Didn't I tell you everything was going to be
fine?' It was my spirit guide, Old Man, talking to me.

My mother sent Rashid and Mohammed to catch one of
the baby goats to make a feast for us. They slaughtered the
little white male goat because he would not give milk. My
mother cut the head off, put it in a basket and very carefully
scraped all the skin off and removed the eyes. The head of
an animal is believed to hold special powers to heal the eyes

and the brain and my mother was praying the entire time she prepared this medicine for my father. She only has one cooking pot and needed that for the rest of the meal so she didn't have anything to cook the head in. She went to the garbage dump and came back with an old can. 'Mama!' I said. 'You can't use an old can from the garbage to cook something in. It's filthy and full of germs. What do you want to do, kill father?'

She looked at me with her hands on her hips. 'I don't really give a care if he dies, he's old and useless anyway, so never mind.'

'Mama, please let me go and borrow one from somebody,' I pleaded.

'No, you are not touching this,' she said shaking her finger in my face. 'I am going to do this, and I'm going to do it my way. Trust me, your father's not going to die from this – he's never going to die, he's too mean.' I could hear my father laughing from behind the house and of course as soon as she said it I realized that the boiling water would kill any germs. 'Child, step out of the way. This is how it's going to cook and he will drink this later,' she said. The can was rusty and she scoured it with clean sand and rinsed it out. She put the goat head inside and filled it with water and some of the special dried leaves she keeps in a small basket to boil on the fire. She tended that head all day long to prepare the special soup for my father.

My mother carefully took the skin off the rest of the goat and saved it to make rope and stools. She dug a hole big enough to hold the animal, and deep enough to hold a fire as well. Nhur and I built a fire with big pieces of wood and when all the wood burned down to white hot coals Mama raked them smooth so she could put the goat on them. She sliced the legs so they could be tucked up close to the body.

You can put whatever you want inside the body of the goat but she put bread, garlic, onions, tomatoes, rice and her special spices. She and Nhur tied it up and placed the meat on top of the glowing coals. Steam and a wonderful smell filled the air and mother knew just when to turn the animal over to the other side so both sides got seared in the fire which keeps the outside dry. Nhur buried it with more glowing coals and ashes from the fire. Mother squatted down next to the fire and fanned it to get the coals hot again, then she shooed everybody away. I was so hungry the smell just about drove me crazy. 'Leave it alone,' she snapped. 'I'll tell you when it's ready. You people are like vultures standing around here.'

When we dug it out the meat was falling apart and melted in my mouth it was so tender. It was absolutely delicious. My father's face was so swollen and painful that he couldn't chew and right before we gathered to eat the goat my mother said his medicine was ready. The goat head had cooked down to a thick gel. She put it into a cup and told me, 'Take this to your father, take it to him.'

I sat down next to him and said, 'OK, Papa, the soup is ready.'

'Is it the same thing that you were fighting over this morning?'

'Yes, Papa. It's good though, it's good for your eyes.'

He said, 'Ah, I don't feel like drinking it now.'

My mother heard that and shouted, 'Hey – what did he say?'

'Mama, he's not going to drink it right now,' I told her.

'What a stinking old man!' she muttered loud enough for the entire camp to hear. 'I made that special medicine and he doesn't want to drink it.' Then she called to me, 'Waris, you bring it right back over here then.' I started to get up but she changed her mind and stated, 'No, you leave it right there. He's not getting anything else until he drinks that.' My father made a pouty mouth like a little baby but sure enough he drank it – the whole thing.

My mother continued haranguing him on her side of the fire, 'Now you are in my land, you hear! You are blind and old and hopeless. You will do whatever I say, you hear me.' What could he do? He had to let her take care of him; he had to drink the special medicine she made for him.

'Who are these other wives? When we went back to Father's house there were three children he said were his,' I asked my mother.

'Well,' she said, 'he says he got rid of one just before you got here. I heard she left him.'

'Why?' I asked. 'What happened?'

'I have no idea why, he doesn't tell me anything,' she said. 'He usually lives with his second wife,' she said matter-of-factly. 'I bet she'll be along to find him and see if you brought her a present.' Mama went back to moving her cooking pots over the fire and it was clear that I wasn't going to hear any more about this from her.

'Burhaan,' I asked, 'Is Father still living with the wife we hung upside down?' I hoped not. I hadn't seen his second wife since my brothers and I hung the poor woman upside down. It had been a big shock when my father came walking back into our camp so many years ago with another wife following behind him. She was not much older than I was but she was not a shy little girl at all. She took over and started ordering my brothers and me around like she was some Somali queen and we were the servants. One day when my father was away, my brothers and I tied her up and hung her from a tree. She behaved much better after that. If my father was still married to her I didn't know what she was going to say if she showed up.

'I don't think she remembers,' said Burhaan.

'How does he manage with three wives?' I asked my brother.

'Once a man had three wives,' he replied. 'They were all jealous of each other so they went to the husband and demanded to know who he loved the best. He told them to close their eyes and he would touch his favorite. The three wives closed their eyes and he touched them all, one after the other.'

Everybody was coming by to meet these relatives from so far away, see what they could get and maybe even say hello. I didn't have any idea what people needed so I brought every kind of thing I could think of – hair creams, soaps, combs, shampoos, toothbrushes and toothpaste. I gave Rashid a blue toothbrush and Colgate toothpaste with fluoride.

'What is this?' he asked.

I said, 'It's called a toothbrush. You put just a little bit of this paste on the bristles and then you brush like this.' I demonstrated with my finger.

He grunted at me and asked, 'Is this the thing that takes all of your gums away and then your teeth fall out?'

'Yes,' I hissed at him, rolling my eyes at the question, 'that's exactly what this does.'

'Well,' he said handing it back to me, 'I already have a *caday* (tooth cleaner),' and he pulled a twig about half an inch thick and three inches long from the pocket of his shirt. 'If you have a toothache this will help. Does the toothbrush do that?'

'No.'

'The camels and goats like to eat this. Can they eat that blue thing?'

'No, this is just for your teeth.'

'Can you eat the stuff in the tube?'

'No, you have to spit it out. It's not good to swallow it.'

'Why do you put something that isn't good for you in your mouth?'

'You just rinse your mouth out with water. It won't hurt you unless you swallow it.'

'Well that is a waste of water. What if you don't have the water to rinse with?'

I didn't have an answer and he went on to explain that when you find a good toothbrush tree you can make tooth cleaners out of the soft new twigs and the older ones are good for spears. You can use the bigger branches for firewood or build a windbreak. The bark on the roots will give you a blister but Mother makes tea from the leaves for people who suffer muscle aches and she grinds them into an antiseptic paste to put on cuts and wounds.

'The seeds contain oil and are edible,' he lectured me. 'When there is nothing else to eat they will keep you alive. Will this toothpaste keep you alive in the dry season?' he asked looking at the little cap with its perfectly formed ridges.

'OK, OK,' I said putting it back in my bag. I gave him a razor but I could tell he was not pleased. I tried to give the toothbrush to Nhur but she also declined.

Burhaan said that the young twigs of the toothbrush tree have resins that kill bacteria in the teeth. 'If you have a stain on your teeth from *khat* or something, we use charcoal to get it off,' he explained and flashed his beautiful teeth at me. They were perfectly white like a light, and lined up in a neat row.

'I know, I know,' I said waving my arms because I was exasperated with all of them. 'I was born here, I know these things. You chew the charcoal, and then you chew a little bit off the end of the Somali tooth stick. You take the tooth stick and rub your teeth with charcoal powder to have the best and whitest teeth.'

'The best teeth you have ever seen,' Rashid said defiantly.

I decided to give the toothbrushes away to some other people. Before I left New York I thought, maybe they need toothbrushes. They don't have dentists and they need to take care of their teeth. Maybe there are no trees and they can't find the tooth stick – I didn't know. I wished I had brought things like shoes and clothes. Food I couldn't bring because it would be spoiled by the time I got there, and that is what they needed most.

That afternoon I sat next to my father, and tried to help him up and fix his pillow and his blanket. I had to put the drops in his eye and I cried when I saw it. It was bruised and swollen with infection. I knew it would be a miracle if he ever opened it again. How could anyone let someone cut his eye open with a knife? It was too much to bear. I gave him some Tylenol for the pain and I was pleased that I had brought it. At least there was one little thing I could do for my father. When I gave him the sandals I brought from New York he felt the leather and ran his finger around the bottom of the thick rubber sole. 'I know who will be able to use these,' he said. 'I'm going to save them for your brother, Rashid,' he said.

When he needed to go to the bathroom someone had to help him because he was weak and unsteady and couldn't see anything. He called for my mother but I said, 'Papa, I'm right here. I'll take you.'

'Are there any shoes around here?' he said.

I found some white flip-flops and put them side by side in front of his feet. 'Let me help you,' I said. 'Give me your hands.'

'No, I'm not that blind. Put the shoes down and I will find them,' he said getting into a squat and feeling around with his toes for the shoes. When he had them on his feet he said, 'Get your mother for me.'

'She's not here, Papa. I don't know where she is.'

'I'll wait for her,' he said and wrapped his arms around his legs.

'I can help you, Papa. I am your child, and I have a child of my own. I can help you,' I told him, but he refused my help. He was not going to listen to me. He just stayed there like a sculpture next to the house waiting for my mother. He sat there for over an hour, proud and stubborn.

I decided to take a nap because I was still tired from all the traveling. I put some mats out and lay down. However, it was impossible to sleep because of everybody coming and going and all the noise. I heard a woman talking to my mother then she walked over to where I was lying down.

'Waris!' she said with a big greeting in her voice. 'How are you?'

Half dazed, I didn't get up. I thought it was somebody who just came by to meet me. I certainly didn't recognize her.

'Waris, you don't remember me do you?' she said, cocking her head to the side like I should know her.

'A lot has changed,' I said. My father was lying there laughing. I looked at her real hard. She looked like she was the same age as my mother.

'Ask your father who I am,' she said.

He said to her, 'How's my baby today?' I wondered what baby he was talking about.

'I'll get him,' she said.

My father lay there and chuckled under his breath until she came back with a little baby in her arms. 'Give me my son,' my father said and then I realized that this was his second wife. She looked like she was as old as my mother but when he first married her, she and I were almost the same age.

I hugged her and said, 'When I left you were having a baby, and now after all these years you are still with a baby.' Dear God I hope she can't remember the time we hung her upside down, I thought. She stayed with us for three nights and never mentioned what we did to her. She had walked for a long way with the baby on her back to get to us. The poor woman was in bad shape; she was hungry and tired. She did not have shoes and her feet were bleeding. That's how I met a brother I hadn't even known about. I have a brother nearly forty years old and I have a brother who is three weeks old.

My father said, 'There is no use living if you have no family and no children.'

I said, 'You know, Father, it's not how many children you have; it's how strong and healthy and how united you are that is more important.'

He said, 'Don't tell me.'

That night around the fire we had a big discussion about men. Burhaan told me that my sister-in-law was asking why I wasn't married.

I said, 'It's not that easy. It's not like one of your camels or goats. You can't buy it and then sell it when you don't want it anymore. Nhur just looked at me and I knew she couldn't understand. That is how they are brought up and that is the only thing that they know – obeying a man. Nhur and her mother asked me if I had a baby.

'Yes, I have a beautiful baby boy,' I told them.

My mother asked, 'Is he anything like you?'

'In every way,' I assured her. She looked at me and rolled her eyes up to Allah. She didn't say anything but 'Uh huh!'

but everybody laughed especially my father. Mama shook her head and said, 'If your child is anything like you, you are going to have some interesting times with him, and you deserve it!'

Nhur said, 'Well, where is his father?'

I said, 'I kicked him out of my life.'

'Why?' they all cried together.

I said, 'Because I had no use for him in my life or my son's life; not at this point anyway.' They all laughed at that, but they were shocked.

'How did you do that?' asked Asha. 'Didn't he kick you out? I thought the man kicked the woman out.'

I said, 'No.'

My sister-in-law stopped laughing and she got very serious. She said, 'We are weak here. The women in this country couldn't do that.'

I said, 'Sister, I was born here. I was raised right here just like you. I learned a lot of great things here, like confidence. I also learned to be self-reliant. I don't sit around and wait for somebody else to do something – I get up and do it. That's what I learned here.' My father was sitting right next to me and my mother came over and joined us. I suppose she wanted to hear what everybody was laughing at. Those women laughed at me saying I learned confidence in Somalia. I said, 'Ask my father and my brothers, they are sitting right here. My brothers know what I am like and what I was like as a child.' I told them, 'Ask my parents, they know exactly what I am and who I am.'

My father joined in and said, 'Oh yes, if she decided to say, "this woman is a rock," there is nothing you could do but let her go. I always thought she was the one with a head like a rock.' Everybody enjoyed that quip, especially my Uncle Ahmed.

'Did you come back to look for a husband?' Nhur said. She just could not believe that I was not married; yet I had money. I was not a beggar.

'No,' I told her. 'I didn't come here to find a husband. I am not married and I have a child but I am not especially looking for a man. When I find one that suits me, then I will think about getting married. That is who I am.' I crossed my arms; I didn't care what they thought.

My father said, 'You are what you are.'

I said to him, 'Do you remember the day you told me, "You aren't one of my children because I don't know where you came from?" You said you had to get rid of me. Do you remember that?'

'I think so,' he said. He looked over in my direction and I could hear the regret in his voice that he once talked to me that way. Every single person was silent and I knew it was because I am the only one of my family who is really standing on her own today. I am very proud of that.

I tried to explain to my father and mother what Guban did to me when I was a small girl. My father asked over and over, 'What did he do?' Neither of my parents remembered anything about that terrible day. I asked if they remembered the afternoon Guban went with me to get the lambs.

'When we were far enough away so nobody could hear he grabbed me and I tried to get away. When I finally broke loose I was covered with sticky smelly stuff.' The words seemed to stick in my mouth. My heart was pounding and I started to sweat. Talking about what Guban did was painful – everyone stared at me and I was too embarrassed to say any more.

My mother shook her head, 'I don't remember him bothering you Waris. What are you talking about?'

'I can't tell you but he was a bad man.'

Father said, 'Child, I don't really even know who you are talking about.' He couldn't remember anybody named Guban and I explained that a relative they took into our home, a person they trusted had attacked me.

My mother said, 'We don't know what happened to you. We haven't seen Guban for many, many years.'

'I hope he's dead and that he went to hell!'

My father and mother were upset that I was so angry with him. 'That's not very nice,' my mother said, stroking my leg to comfort me. 'What are you saying?'

I finally decided that there was no point in going back over it again. Words about such a taboo subject would not come out with my father and mother sitting right there. Maybe a *djinn* slides into your mouth and sits on your tongue. 'You don't know but he did something very bad,' I finally said and everyone became very quiet. I wanted desperately to tell them exactly what happened, but I couldn't. We don't talk about such things – ever. However, the long silence was strangely comforting. At least my parents understood that Guban did a terrible thing to their daughter. The worst emotional pain is to be sexually violated and have everyone ignore it. Nobody said anything for a long time and Mama patted my leg with a worried face. She kept looking into my eyes to read their secrets and what she saw troubled her, but she wouldn't ask – we don't talk about such things. If you aren't allowed to talk about sex, you better sew the girls shut because then, like me, they won't know what is happening to them.

Sometimes great pain is a great gift and I believe that Allah had given me a gift. I knew now where to start with my campaign to eliminate female genital mutilation. Women had to be educated about sex. Men needed to know about women's bodies as well as their own.

My little cousin Amina interrupted my thoughts, 'Could you take a letter for me to America?'

'America is a big place. I have to have an address.'

Her eyes filled with anxiety and she twisted her dress between her fingers. 'I have the address and I will give it to you.'

'Who lives there?' I asked, curious about who she knew.

'My husband is there,' she said quietly, not even looking into my eyes.

'What is your husband doing there?' I asked her, shaking my head. She mumbled something and I thought she couldn't have any idea what he was doing there. 'How long have you been married?'

She said, 'Four years.' I couldn't believe it; she looked like she was only sixteen.

'Do you have children?'

'No. He chose me and left me. I hope he'll come back and take me to wherever he is.'

I told her 'Don't wait for him!' Several people gasped and my mother shook her head and clicked her tongue against the roof of her mouth in disapproval. I agreed to take the letter. I didn't want to make any more trouble.

My family found most of my ideas upsetting or funny. My cousin said, 'Waris, you talk like a man and you act like you are very strong.'

'You can be strong too. Look, I was raised here just like you.' They all laughed at me again. I felt like I was the local comedy act. Everywhere I went people followed me. Basically I decided it was for two reasons. First because they thought I was rich, and second because they thought I was crazy and different. Despite all that I felt proud and grateful to be in my village and I was so glad I made it. I thanked Allah again and again. It was a miracle to find not only my mother but my brothers and all these cousins, nephews and other relatives I never even knew I had.

One of the most important things to me was that I was face to face with my father and feeling equal. I couldn't agree with some of what he said and I carefully explained what I thought. He asked questions when he didn't understand what I said. I educated him and he was pleased. He kept joking, 'Are you sure this is my daughter?' 'Who are you?' he repeated over and over. 'I thought my daughter was dead and gone a long time ago.'

'Why?'

'When a little girl runs away from her father what good can happen? The only things that you knew were your camels and your goats. First I thought that you were killed and eaten by lions and the hyenas sucked out the marrow in your bones. Then I heard you were in Mogadishu and London so I assumed you must be a prostitute. What else could you do? You went so far it's like you traveled to another *hydigi*, another planet, all by yourself. Child, you are alive and you are able to make a living all by yourself! You are talking with power and dignity.'

My father was proud of me; he was proud of me! That made me feel strong, passionate about life, and proud of myself. Once I was the little girl my father used to beat. If he noticed me at all he would say, 'Hey you! Get that for me. Hurry up!' I was terrified of him. When he could see me with his eyes, he saw a girl of no consequence. Now my father could see with the eyes of his heart. *Allah Bah Wain*, God is Great.

11

desert life

A daughter is not a guest

African Proverb

Every afternoon for the next several days it rained with heavy drops gushing out of gray clouds. Everyone watched the clouds gather and fill the sky all afternoon, waiting for the rain. The *gu* or rainy season took over the village and changed everything, but nobody complained. The hot, hot weather was gone, cooled off by the blessing of water. The town had a river running down the middle of the street where dust blew a few days before. My mother's little hut was totally flooded. Everything was soaked, even the poor little goats. They didn't know what to do and hid in the house, shaking and wet right to the ends of their brown tails. My brother, Burhaan, dug a trench around his house to try and keep the water from going inside. Everybody was smiling and happy because we love the rain so much. The little babies sat and played in the muddy water and sad to say, kept drinking it too. I knew they would soon be sick from diarrhea and be shitting all over the place. Women gathered water in the streets and poured their little buckets into bigger containers so the dirt would settle to the bottom and the water could be used for cooking and bathing.

We got up each day around six o'clock with the roosters crowing and the birds starting to gossip and the chickens squabbling about this and that. There were no lights after the sun dropped below the distant horizon and closed its eyes so everybody went to bed early and got up with the sun. There was not much to do at night and sometimes the shops ran out of oil for the lamps. It seemed like supplies were erratic, I suppose due to the dangerous conditions around Mogadishu.

Mohammed was sleeping at my uncle's house, and it was crowded there. Of course in this little village, there were no hotels or extra places to stay. Everything was used all the time. When someone came for a visit, everybody moved over a little bit to make room.

'Did you sleep well?' I said.

Mohammed brushed his hand in the air like he was swatting a fly. 'The next time we come back I want to have the extra room on Burhaan's house finished so we can all sleep together,' he said. Mohammed went into Mama's house to fill her yellow plastic pot with water to wash, bumping his head on the low door. He sat on a low stool in the courtyard, took off his glasses, carefully placed them on a rock and washed his face and arms. He took a little water in his hand and rubbed it all over his face and up and down his bare arms then he faced the sun for a moment to dry. He took off his right shoe and sock and washed his foot, and then he put them back on so he could balance while he did the other.

I noticed that all the trees and bushes had a wisp of light green color and only a few days ago they had seemed defeated and dead. My skin believes that all of the shrubs in Somalia have thorns. They need every bit of life they have and in the *jilaal* or dry season, the sharp thorns say, 'Stay away, I have nothing for you.' When it rains the leaves grow very quickly, everything is full of joy.

I didn't especially enjoy using the local bathroom. My mother does not have her own, you have to share, and you could smell it before you saw it. It was a small square room less than four feet on each side with a latch-less wooden door and open to the sky. In the middle of the cement floor was a small square hole. You squat over the hole and do your business, which falls into a deep hole. It smelled serious; the floor was wet and dirty and I was in and out as quick as I could be. People walked barefoot over rocks and through thorn bushes but not to the bathroom. If you didn't have any shoes you waited until somebody walked by with a pair you could borrow.

On the way back I saw some little village boys watching me. One boy had skin as black as I ever saw gleaming in the sunshine. 'Oh Blackie, Blackie,' I called to him. 'Give me your beautiful skin!' I got my camera to take some pictures of them and I also wanted to film my family. The boys danced around and smiled when they weren't staring at me. They posed for the camera with beautiful white teeth framed by lovely black faces. Every single child wore a protective leather amulet around their neck. Allah was everywhere.

Taking pictures of my family was a different matter. As soon as Mohammed saw me come back to the house with my camera, he started shouting at everyone, 'Do not let her take pictures of you until you're dressed up. Don't let her photograph you looking like that, she is going to sell the pictures to the magazines!' He would not stop sticking out his tongue at the camera and waving his hands so I couldn't get a good shot. Burhaan got up and went inside his house and wouldn't come back out. He looked out through the metal bars over his windows and backed away whenever I raised the camera to take his picture.

I shouted at them, 'Don't be ridiculous. I'm not selling your picture to any fashion magazines! Come on, I am just taking a few snapshots for myself. I want to show them to my friends. Come back out here, you guys.' I gave up on the boys and turned to my mother, 'Mama, mama, let me take your picture. I just want to have a picture of you to take back with me.'

Mohammed said, 'No, no, she is going to sell it to some magazine for the cover, I guarantee you!' Everybody thought he was serious. He told them to put on their best clothes and wash so they wouldn't be dusty and dirty in the pictures. 'If she takes a picture of you all dusty, beat her up! Break the camera,' he told them.

I stood right in front of my pesky brother and shouted at him, 'Mohammed! You're crazy and you know it. Stop telling them that.'

'No, no,' he said, enjoying the game. He pointed at me and repeated like he was some big authority on the subject, 'She's going to the fashion magazines.'

Finally I told them, 'You people look like a bunch of refugees! You know that. The only place I'm going to sell your picture is The National Geographic! I'm serious.' I couldn't believe they were giving me so much trouble over a little family snapshot I would get developed at the drugstore. '*Hoyo*, Mother,' I pleaded, 'please let me take your picture.'

'I'm busy,' she said. She never stopped; she was always doing something from early in the morning before anyone else even got up, until late at night.

'*Hoyo*,' I begged, 'please sit still. I want some pictures of you to show my son. I want him to know his grandmother and family.'

'Well then, take the picture,' she snapped, standing like a stick.

Rashid stood in front to block my shot and said, 'Mama, you have to put on some other dress for a picture.'

'I already got dressed this morning,' Mama said.

He snatched at her ragged brown dress and insisted, 'Go put on the one I bought for you. You can't wear this old thing in a picture.'

Mama muttered at him to leave her alone but she went inside her house and came out wearing another dress over the top of the old brown one. It had deep purple stripes and yellow flowers. She is so thin that it didn't show that she was wearing everything she owned. Suddenly she was shy and put her *chalmut* over her face while I snapped the camera shutter. Mohammed sat on his three-legged stool and kept ordering everybody around, as usual. He told her you had to stick out your tongue in pictures and of course she listened to him.

'Burhaan,' I pleaded. 'Help me take some pictures of *Aba*.' Burhaan and Mohammed went to get him. They supported him between them and walked him carefully out into the sun so he would not trip.

'Oh, it's the beautiful Dirie family,' I said with the video camera rolling. I noticed that my father was not as tall as Mohammed anymore. When *Aba* realized that I was taking a picture of him supported by my brothers he pushed both of them away from him and stood alone, erect and dignified even with a bandage covering one eye and the other blind. He would not have his picture taken leaning on somebody. He looked like the powerful father I knew as a child. Nothing could take the strength in his spirit from him.

Nhur was eight months pregnant but every day she walked all the way into town to get clean drinking water from the only supply. It was a standpipe and you could fill your jug for ten shillings. She carried six gallons back by herself. She filled two jugs and carried one in each hand. I saw her coming over the hill with the two jugs of water. She went a little way then stopped to rest and catch her breath. I ran to help her as soon as I saw her. Meanwhile my brothers sat around the house talking and arguing about politics. I said to her, 'Where is that useless husband of yours? Doing nothing. Why do you allow this?' She just gave me a look.

When Nhur came back from the well she walked to the village market in the heat to see what food was available that day. She bought rice wrapped in cones made of old newspaper and goat meat if she could find it. She bought spices wrapped in squares of paper; just enough for the day's pot of food, not a whole bottle. She gathered wood and built a cooking fire. She cut the meat into pieces and carefully removed the fat and bad parts. She cooked the rice and meat with a little oil, an onion or two and some tomato. She kept fanning the fire to keep it hot. When it was done, she piled the rice in the center of a round tin tray and made an indentation in the middle where she put the goat meat in its spicy sauce. She served the men the platter of rice with tea made with a little ghee. She cleaned the cooking pots while the men were eating. When they were finished she brought whatever was left over into the cooking area and only then did she eat with the children.

The first day I arrived Nhur's mother walked into the village from the desert encampment where she lived. She came back every day after that. She was one of the most beautiful women I have ever seen. She had green eyes and stood even taller than me. Her eyes and nose were evenly spaced and the shape of her face was a perfect oval but the woman had a faded rag for a dress, and I never saw her wear anything else. It might have been orange or red at one time, but it was so old it looked mostly gray. It must have been the only thing she had to put on her body. She, like most Somalis, was a proud woman and she would never, ever ask for anything. We fed her every day without a question because that is the way things are in my country.

I decided I had seen enough of this and the next day I told my sister-in-law, 'Nhur, I'll cook today. You go and visit with your beautiful mother. Nhur flashed me a smile and said she would get some water. She wrapped her blue *chalmut* over her head and took the water jugs. I put a bunch of wood on the fire to build it up and stuck the biggest pot I could find on top of it. It would not balance so I pushed the pot down hard and made a place for it in the wood so it wouldn't fall over. I filled it up with rice and beans and added water to the top.

The fire started to smoke because the wood was all wet from the rain. We didn't have any dry wood – there wasn't any place to keep it dry. I tried to fan it to get it burning hot again but it kept smoking and smoking. I was coughing and the smoke was getting in my eyes and burning me every time the wind shifted. I figured I did something wrong with the fire but I hadn't cooked on a fire in twenty years. Forever, really, because I didn't do a lot of cooking before I left Somalia. We don't have open cooking fires in New York City or London. I called Burhaan, 'Hey, come on over and help me with this would you?' I asked. He's been around a lot more fires than I have.

'That's women's work,' he said, sitting on the mats in the shade.

'Hey,' I said, 'I need some help over here.'

'Get Nhur to help you,' he said. 'Cooking is women's work.' He just watched me struggle and was totally unwilling to lend a hand because cooking is so-called women's work. He had nothing to do but sit there but he was still not going to help. I wanted to take off my shoe and beat him.

'Mohammed, don't you be as ridiculous as Burhaan,' I said. 'Get up and fix this fire or we won't eat.'

'That is not my problem. We do the men stuff,' he said.

'Like, what is the men stuff?' I stood up and asked. 'If something needs to be done, what is this, you do this, I can only do that business?' I threw a stick at the two of them and Mohammed threw it back at me, laughing. 'I don't see it,' I said. 'Would you sit there and starve if you didn't have a woman to cook for you?'

'No,' Burhaan laughed. 'We would just get the children to cook.' Finally Nhur came back with more water, walking slowly with her big baby belly. She put the water down and lifted that heavy pot off the fire. She poked the sticks around and positioned them differently. She put bigger sticks on either side and balanced the pot on top. Then she squatted down in front of the fire and fanned it back to life.

'One of the things that has ruined this country is *khat*,' I said to my brothers.

'We don't have any *khat* today,' Rashid said.

'If you could get it you would be chewing it,' I said. I hated that he had started that horrid habit. 'Men don't have any motivation,' I told them. 'They are not using their minds and they are wasting their lives sitting around chewing a ridiculous weed.'

After we ate I went to be with my mother. We were sitting in her little hut talking because it was raining outside. My aunt got up to go outside to the bathroom and I said, 'Can I hold him?' so she left me with her little baby. He looked just like me and we connected. He wouldn't cry if I held him. When we talked he would look me right in the eyes.

Mama went to get a little bit of goat milk she was saving for him in a cup. In Somalia we don't have baby bottles or cups. You just take the child's cheeks and gently squeeze them together then hold the cup up and carefully adjust it so the baby can suck on the edge of the cup. My nephew had such an itty-bitty perfect little mouth. I was happy to feed him but I heard my mother muttering under her breath.

She was talking to herself as she got the milk, 'Oh my God, don't leave the baby with her,' she said. 'Is she going to feed the baby? Does she know what she is doing?' She wasn't saying it to anyone, just talking to herself out loud.

I looked at her and said, 'Mama, what do you think I am? Am I that hopeless? Don't you know I am a mother myself?'

'*Hiiyea*,' she acknowledged.

'Like I am thirty something years old.'

'*Hiiyea*.'

'Didn't you raise me here?'

My mother looked at me and she said, 'Oh yes, that's right,' but she said it like she had no confidence in me.

I said, 'Come over and sit next to me. I am offended by what you said.' She gave me the cup and I took the baby's face and gently placed my opened fingers around his mouth while I held him close. He drank it without spilling one precious drop.

She said, 'Ah child, I didn't mean it like that. I thought

you lived so differently that you forgot what to do with the children.'

I had to think why she said that before I answered her. I thought she probably thinks I forgot everything I learned and what she taught me. Maybe that is what she is thinking. I said, 'Mama, I raised my own child myself and I fed him the way you taught me. You taught me how to feed a baby. This is something that I will never forget because you showed me. Please don't think that I don't know how to take care of children properly.'

'I'm sorry, Waris,' she said looking at me sideways. I think my mother was pleased with me. Even though we had a little fight, she could see that I valued her ways, and the things she taught me. I didn't forget the important things because I lived in a different place.

I am a very self-reliant person because of where I grew up. I learned how to do a lot of things most people don't do, like cutting hair so I tried to cut my baby brother's hair. There were no barbers in town and Rashid complained that his was getting too long.

'Father keeps asking me why I am hanging around here. I have to get back to the animals,' he said. 'I can't sit around and wait for a barber to show up.'

But when I picked up the scissors everyone said, 'Ah, no, no!'

I asked, 'What do you mean?'

They said, 'You can't do that.'

I said, 'I know how to cut hair. You can trust me.'

'No, Waris, that's not the point,' my father said flatly and waved his finger in the air.

'Well, what's the point then?'

'You can't have a woman cut a man's hair.'

'What are you talking about?' I said, totally exasperated

with them again. 'What difference does it make who cuts his hair? Are the camels going to notice?'

They all cried, 'He would be laughed at.'

I said, 'Who is going to laugh at him? You? Are you that way?'

'Don't worry, he's going to be laughed at,' my father insisted.

I found it hard to accept and I argued, 'As long as I know how to cut hair, and I have the intelligence to do it, what's the problem?'

My father said, 'That is not the real reason, Waris. That is just the way things are here.'

I said, 'Papa, don't insult my intelligence, please. It's not like I don't know the system, like I don't know the culture.' This is the clash we always had. I asked him and all my brothers, 'So when are you going to change?' I told them, 'It's like this circumcision thing with women. The women are ready to change.' A silence fell over the room like a cloud covering the sun. I knew that they would not discuss this in mixed company, if at all. 'You let me take your pictures,' I said, changing the subject. 'Yet a lot of people here believe that will steal your spirit.'

'Only ignorant people still believe that,' Burhaan said.

'Why is a woman cutting a man's hair different than that?'

I tried and tried to reason with them but I got nowhere. I could provoke them all I wanted, they were not going to change the way they did things. Still I could not get angry. I was so happy to be sitting in front of a hut with my mother, my father, my brothers and people I have not seen in so very long. I said, 'This is a dream I've been dreaming for thirty years. At least I think I'm almost thirty years old, I don't know.'

My father raised his head up and said, 'I think you are nearly forty.' Mohammed and I cracked up.

My mother said, 'No she's not. Burhaan is around twenty-seven years old and he follows her by two years or so.' Her voice trailed off because she didn't know how old any of us were any more than my father did.

I didn't care that dates were not important to my parents. Here I was under the stars of a beautiful African night. I forgot how many stars there are in the sky or maybe they had star babies while I was gone for so many years. It was so clear I felt like I could reach up and milk the sky. It's true what they say; there is no feeling like it – there is no feeling like home. Oh how I missed that feeling of belonging to something much greater than myself. I regretted that I hadn't been there for so many years. I had not seen my people age and grow old. I had not been there when they needed me. My father said, 'Don't worry about me, it's only age Waris, I am still strong. Tomorrow I am going to find me another big wife and have a couple more children to take care of the goats.' I loved that he was still cracking jokes and I realized how much I had missed my father and how much I cared about him. I pretended to be tough at one point and said, 'You did this to me, you made me run away,' but I wouldn't change a thing, not one thing in my life. I have said that before and I will say it again. I wish I could bring the time back but there is no regret in my mind. We all stumble through life and even though I didn't have a pair of shoes to cushion my rocky path, I don't regret the path I walked. Some parts have been hard; some things have been wonderful, but it is all experience and everything has a time and a place. I used to dream and wish that my father and mother and my sister and my brothers were in one place because I never had that. Now I had this one amazing week with my family. It was a dream that I wished for my whole life and I thanked Allah it came true.

12

somali education

To bear a girl is to bear a problem

Somali Saying

My mother's little village was full of people who left Mogadishu to find somewhere safe to live. They were running away from stray bullets and the constant battles for control in the streets. The village had grown like a column of army ants. There was not enough water, no electricity, no doctors, no medical dispensary and the nearest hospital was over a hundred miles away. When I asked about schools for the children Ragge told me 'I teach.'

Curious, I asked him, 'Where? I didn't know there was a school in this little place.'

'Come on and I'll show you,' he told me. Last year Ragge and a clansman from Mogadishu decided to put together a school. They got enough money from the United Nations Children's Fund to build one square room with a tin roof and a dirt floor. They opened a school for the children in the village. Ragge was educated in Mogadishu where my uncle was once a businessman. He knew how to read in Somali, Arabic, Italian and English. He didn't have a job so he thought, well, at least I can teach the children. His English was excellent and I enjoyed talking to him.

He said, 'Tomorrow morning I'll stop by and pick you up on my way to the school. Be ready.'

'OK, I'll be ready,' I said, eager to support him and the school in whatever way I could.

The next morning the goats still had long shadows when he came and called to me in the house, 'Are you ready?'

'Of course,' I replied and came outside to go with him. Every day the sun beamed down so strong that I got up early, very early. By six o'clock I already had breakfast and was dressed and ready to go. Nobody knows or cares what time it is because the sun gets you up and gets you moving and the dark puts you to sleep at night.

When I ducked my head and came out of the little hut my mother was sitting there cleaning her teeth with her tooth stick. She took it out of her mouth and said, 'Where does she think she's going?' She snatched at my dress as if it was an old rag.

I said, 'What? Mama – what's the matter with what I'm wearing?' My dress was the one I wore around the house. It was a long Somali *dirah* with a white petticoat underneath. I held a scarf that I borrowed from Dhura in Amsterdam. She kept shaking her head and I took my dress out of her hands and said, 'Who am I dressing for? I'm just going over to the school.'

My mother rolled her eyes and put both hands up in the air as if I had on a mini-skirt. She waved her palms in my face. 'I don't know where you came from girl, but you are not stepping out of the house looking like that. No, you are not shaming me with this dress.'

What was so shameful in what I had on? I wailed, 'Mama, look, I am all covered up.' I put the scarf on my head and turned around to show her that I was properly covered from head to toe.

She said, 'Get back in the house and get dressed nicely to go to the school.'

I said, 'What is the problem? Would you mind telling me what is the problem with what I am wearing?' Nhur and my mother were both shouting at me and acting like I had offended the Prophet Mohammed himself. They told me the color was tacky, the scarf didn't match, and to put on my nice dress. They acted like I was going to meet the queen or the president. I couldn't believe all this fuss. 'You've got to be kidding me! Getting dressed up is one thing that I know. Do you know Gucci? Have you ever heard of Armani? One of those dresses could feed this village for a week.'

'Why would you eat a dress?' Nhur asked and I realized that there was no way they could understand. I have talked to hundreds of people all over the world and been on television. I know how to dress! My own family treated me like a stupid, ignorant child and it was hopeless for me to protest. I had to listen to people who were sharing two pairs of flip-flops and had never used a napkin or been in an elevator. Ragge just stood there looking the other way. He was not going to get into the middle of this, no matter how he felt.

My mother insisted, 'No, you have to change.' She took my hands and gently led me back inside her little hut. In Somalia even a woman suffering from malnutrition will dress in the best things she can and carry herself regally. How you dress and carry yourself is all they worry about. I was concerned with getting people clean water, proper medical care and good schools; what did my dress mean? However, when my mother is determined, you will listen and do what she tells you. I had to take off the cool cotton *dirah* and put on my best one with the embroidered petticoat and the slippery silk scarf that matched. Mother said, 'Yes, put that one on, wear that one, the other one looked like you were some kind of woman without a good family or something.'

It was already getting hot as the sun climbed up over the house and I was sweating. Worried that I would make Ragge late for school I ripped everything off and dug through my suitcase to find my good dress. Then I had to get dressed all over again being careful not to let anything fall on the dirt floor of the tiny little hut. I could barely stand up straight inside and the sun beat through the tin roof making it into an oven.

Mama was not satisfied until I put on the silk scarf that would not stay on my head no matter how I tried to drape it. It had to be tied tightly around my neck for fear it would slip off and get dirty in the mud. When I went back outside another chorus of 'No, no, that dress is see through!' greeted me. 'Are you crazy? Put something under the top. Do you have a T-shirt?'

Putting my foot down I said, 'No, I don't want to put one on because it's too hot. I'm already sweating and it's still early.'

My three brothers showed up out of nowhere. They came around the corner, three tall men, arm in arm. Whenever you need them they are never around, but suddenly they were all over the place like a pack of hyenas nipping at me from every direction. 'Hey, what is she doing!' they all said.

Mohammed got very official like he was the boss of everybody. 'No, no you can't go like that,' he told me shaking his head. Everybody was all over me, all over again. I gave up and put on everything they told me just to get out of there.

Ragge was laughing and laughing as we walked through the village to the school. I told him to cut it out or I wasn't even going to go to his darn school and that made him whoop he laughed so hard. My official visit dressed up in my very best outfit was to one brick room with two holes cut out for windows, a flimsy wooden door, a dirt floor and covered by a flat tin roof. I looked fabulous.

There must have been a hundred children of all ages running and chasing each other all around. Ragge and his friend, Ali, who said he was the headmaster, were in charge of the school. Ragge clapped his hands and shouted to the children, 'Get in line, it's time to go in for school.' They don't start at some pre-determined time that it says on a clock; school begins whenever the teachers get there. The children immediately started to line up and go inside. The girls looked like flowers with bright blue and yellow dresses and red scarves. Most of them had dresses made from the same pattern, it was probably the only cloth in town. One of the girls had a round face like a ball and ears that stuck out to the side. She looked at me shyly and gave me the biggest smile when she passed by like she admired me. She reminded me of myself as a child because she was bold enough to look me right in the eyes and I loved her for that. I was amazed that somebody thought I was somebody! Most of the boys wore what looked to me like old school uniforms; white shirts with blue piping at the collars and cuffs. Several boys had on long blue pants that were so big on their skinny bones they dragged in the dirt. It was a wonder they didn't trip over them like I did on my dress. There were so many children that they were packed like bees in a hive. I thought, let them all settle down and then

I will go in and say good morning. I stood in front of the
door and watched them all sit down together right on the
dusty floor. They didn't have one single chair or table or
even a book in the whole place. The kids sat on the dirt. A
few had a thin cloth, but most were right on the packed
earth floor. All those pairs of shining eyes looked up, they
were so eager to learn but they had no materials to help
them. I was proud that my cousin was trying to teach them.
I could not understand why my father and brothers didn't
trust Ragge. He didn't sit around all day complaining about
how things were, he was trying to do something, trying to
make a difference.

Ragge talked to the students and used a big stick to point
at words. They didn't have a proper chalkboard but he had
painted some of the wooden boards black. Every one of
those sweet little children was listening to every single thing
he said. They didn't even notice me taking pictures; they
were so eager to learn. They watched the teacher as if he
were a baby goat and they were hungry lions. Some of the
boys were so intent they chewed on their pencil but most of
the babies had absolutely nothing! If a child had a pencil
and a piece of paper, that child was very rich. It was very sad
for me to look at that and to think about the kids in my
neighborhood who would rather hang around the street
than go to school and learn something. I always wanted to
go to school, to learn to read books easily and write and
spell perfectly but I never had the chance. I have been working my whole life to support myself. I never had the
opportunity to sit in a classroom and listen to a teacher.
Everything I know I taught myself. Standing there I forgot
about being hot and uncomfortable; school is a magic place
for me.

Ragge asked if I would like to say hello to the children. 'I am so happy to meet you,' I said. 'School is a wonderful place and you are so lucky to have a teacher.' The children all wanted to know where I lived and I tried to tell them something about New York City. 'There are buildings so high you almost can't see the top. The streets are full of cars and they are all covered up with cement so there is no grass.'

Hands shot up and one of the boys asked, 'What do the goats eat?'

'There are no goats in New York.'

'How do you get milk to drink?' they all wanted to know.

I asked if anyone would like to come and live in New York and sad to say, almost every hand went up. The children were eager to leave Somalia, to get to the West even though they knew nothing about it – they just assumed it would be better than Somalia.

I asked the headmaster who built the building. He told me that UNICEF gave the village elders enough money to buy the bricks and the tin. The fathers worked together to build the school for their children. Ali showed me a sign on the front of the building from UNICEF. Already it was too crowded and more children lined up every morning. I asked him how the teachers were paid and he told me that they were lucky to get thirty dollars a month but they had not been paid for a long time. 'Somebody comes around with money every so often but I don't know if there is a Somali Ministry of Education any more, or if the funding is from the United Nations or where it comes from,' he told me.

'How can you get by without getting paid?'

'Teachers live because everybody helps everybody. If you go to somebody's house and they have food you don't have to ask for it; they will share whatever they have with you. Food is not what I worry about. Without a salary I can't

build a life. I can't have a home of my own or get married or
have children. See if you can help us,' Ali asked me. 'We
don't get paid and we don't have any books or other supplies. Anything would help us.'

After I came out of the school I noticed that an old roos-
ter was strutting around the school yard and crowing like he
was the one in charge. He pecked importantly at the ground
looking for a seed in the dust. I don't think anybody else
noticed him and I feel that way about my country. People in
the West don't notice my poor little country.

Nhur kept saying, 'We have to do some henna to celebrate your visit. You can't go home without henna,' she said.
I was looking forward to it. It's an ancient tradition that cel-
ebrates a woman's beauty. Henna is a symbol of joy and is
applied for your wedding night, or after you have a baby, to
welcome the child to life. If a woman is very sick and is
healed by God we will use henna to celebrate her return to
life. Women may also apply it when they are going out to a
celebration.

'Could you do it for me?' I asked Nhur but she declined.
She wanted to wait for her cousin or two particular neighbors to do it. I didn't know when or if they would show up so
I said, 'Let's not wait for them. You do it.' I just assumed that
she could do henna designs as well as anybody, she lived in
the village her whole life. I did notice that she wasn't wearing any, and Mama wasn't wearing any. Henna designs only
last for about ten days so the darker and the deeper the
color the better. Nhur and I went to the market one afternoon and brought back some henna. She mixed the powder
with warm water, added a little bit of oil and stirred it into a
paste. You let it sit for about ten minutes, then it is ready.
Nhur picked up a stick and started to draw a design on my
calf, down to my foot. The more she drew the more the

designs started to all run together into a big puddle. I said, 'Hey, what's going on?'

Nhur explained that she really didn't know how to do henna designs. I didn't want to make her feel bad so I reassured her that it was OK. She carefully drew another henna design on the other leg and we had a nice talk. I offered her some oranges from the market but Nhur said she didn't want to eat them. 'I was so hungry when I was pregnant with Aleeke that I ate all the time,' I told her.

Nhur gave me a sad look. 'I don't want to eat so the baby won't get too big. I had a very difficult time when my daughter was born. They had to cut me open so that she could come out and sew the incision back up again.'

What could I say? I shook my head and patted her hand. I know the birth of a child is a big worry when you are infibulated. How will the baby be born when the opening is so small. 'I will pray that everything goes well for you,' I told her.

Nhur sang a little *hoobeyo*, or woman's song while she drew the designs. We always sing about our problems.

> *Oh my daughter, men have wronged us*
> *In a dwelling where there are no women*
> *No camels are milked*
> *Nor are the saddled horses mounted.*

After Nhur finished the designs on my arms and hands I went outside to sit in the sun, and let it dry. I was hot and I didn't want my henna to get all messed up while I was frying in the sun, so I took off my scarf and slip. I didn't want to sit in the sun all covered with clothes; I wanted to get a little tan. I pulled up my dress and tucked it under me and rolled up the sides to my shoulders. I sat with my arms and legs

stretched out to that wonderful Somali sun like a lizard.
Sorry to say my foot looked like I had stepped into red
paint – like a cow's foot, but I didn't care. It felt so wonderful to be cared for and to be cared about by Nhur. It was a
blessing from a sister-in-law I had grown to love.

Just as I got comfortable my brother Mohammed walked
by and said, 'What! Did they lock her out of the little hut?'

My mother and Nhur heard him and they both rushed
out shouting, 'Oh my God! Look at that, she has her dress
up to her waist. Cover her up, cover her! What is she doing
now?'

I looked up at the three of them dancing around like
chickens chased by a dog. I said, 'Nhur, why don't you come
over here because I'm going to slap you! You have given me
enough problems already today.'

'Waris, you can't sit outside like this,' Nhur said shaking
her head.

'Leave me alone you crazy woman,' I told her. 'What are
you all worried about? Who is coming by this little hut and
who is going to see? See what?'

I was laughing and they were sighing and saying, 'Oh she
never changed, only she's worse now. She's even crazier
than she was. She won't even listen now.'

Later that afternoon two women came by to visit with
Nhur. I noticed that they had the most beautiful henna
designs on their hands and feet. 'Who did these for you?' I
asked. 'They are wonderful flowers and symbols.'

'We did it ourselves,' they said.

'Where do you live?' I asked.

'Right next door.'

Nhur said, 'These are the neighbors I wanted to do your
henna, but you wanted me to do it.'

13

ummi

Ummi — An Arabic word meaning illiterate – untouched by knowledge from any source other than God

My mother, bless her heart, she won't stop. The day before we had to leave she disappeared for a long time. I looked for her all over the village and asked Mohammed, Rashid and Burhaan where she was. When Nhur came back from the outdoor market she told me Mama left before the chickens were up and squawking. Nhur pointed west into blue hills near the border with Ethiopia. When the sun's bottom squatted on the village I saw a tiny figure in the distance balancing a big load on her back. She looked like a *djinn* or a fire-spirit because the heat danced in waves all around her. Mama had gathered sticks and a huge dead branch, wrapped the dusty things in her *chalmut,* and tied it with a big knot. No wonder her headscarf was a rag! She used it to carry everything from goats to firewood. She lifted that heavy load and carried it from the other side of the horizon on her back. She had a five-gallon plastic jug in each hand filled with water. The wood wasn't enough; she had to get water at the well and carry that back too in the hottest part of the day.

I ran out to meet her and help her with that heavy load. 'Mama,' I shouted to her, 'why didn't you tell me where you were going? I would have helped you.'

She just shrugged and laughed at me, 'You were sleeping.'

'Mama!' I shouted and made her give me the water jugs. She looked at me with her funny smile and kept on walking. My mother is tougher than any three people I know. She has looked for wood every day of her life. While I have been strutting on the fashion runways in Paris and Milan she has been gathering the wood that Allah provides and sending smoke back up to Him.

Mother lifted the firewood off her back and talked to Nhur about what she found in the *suq* that morning. Some days there is very little to buy, even if you have money, and there hadn't been any meat that morning. Usually the skinned carcass of a goat or a sheep will hang on a nail to prove that it was properly slaughtered. The seller brushes the flies off and cuts out the part of the meat you want to buy – rib, shoulder, or leg. Each cut has a different price. Today, nothing had been available. My mother had carried wood back for a big fire, but we didn't have anything to cook but rice and goat milk. *Hoyo* called my brother Rashid. When I asked him to do something he argued with me, but when my mother said his name, he came to her immediately. She told him to go and get the last one of her baby goats. 'Go and find *Ourgi Yeri*, Little Baby,' she said and gestured in the direction of the termite mounds.

'What are you going to do with the pretty baby goat?' I

asked, but she ignored me and started building up the fire. *Ourgi Yeri*'s knees were black and brown against his white body, like he knelt in the mud to say prayers. 'Mama,' I pleaded, 'you don't need to do that. I don't have to eat meat, believe me I don't. Don't kill your baby goat because I'm here. Keep it for yourself! Please, Mama, I really don't care about meat.'

'Sometimes that is how life is, Waris,' Mama replied, firmly. She has so much faith that it spills over and fills up those around her. She believes that God will provide for her and I stopped my chatter.

Rashid didn't question her and he took the long slaughtering knife with him. Goats don't need much care in the rainy season when there are plenty of green shoots nearby for them to nibble on. Rashid quickly caught *Ourgi Yeri* and carried him in his arms to the back of the hut. Burhaan helped get him on his knees with his neck outstretched. The poor little thing knew something was up and he bleated and struggled. I couldn't watch them kill it, he was such a pretty animal. They needed to slaughter it properly or my family would not eat the meat. It was critical to slit his throat so that he would die quickly and without pain. That is the Muslim way.

It was upsetting because my mother loved that goat. Every morning she snuggled up to him and scratched him under his chin where a little beard was beginning to sprout. Those goats were everything to her, and no wonder – they provided milk and that was often the only thing she had to eat or give her family. The animals provided white nourishment to my brother's family, to little Mohammed, and to my mother's neighbors as well. Now she slaughtered the last young goat to feed her family. Mama gave whatever little thing she had without a thought for tomorrow.

Suddenly everything was silent and you could hear doves cooing on the neighbor's house. Mama was, of course, stoic, only she looked up at the soft hills for a minute. For me, hunger has a human face and it is my mother's. She only had five goats in this world, and three were left because we ate the two babies while we were there.

Rashid brought the goat's carcass to my mother, its head in a tightly woven conical basket. Mama took the knife and sharpened it on a stone. She skinned and gutted the goat. She set aside the hide to make a three-legged stool by stretching the wet hide over the legs for a seat. As it dries it will shrink tight and firm. Mama carefully cut up every single piece of that animal including its eyes, nose and lips. She gave the two little horns to Mohammed *Inyer* to play with; the meat went into her cooking pot. Mohammed *Inyer* danced around with the horns. He blew into them to see if he could make a sound and gaily tooted in my mother's face. Then he started to dig with one of them and the dust blew into her meat. 'Get away from my cooking pot or I'll take those back and wear them myself,' she said flicking her knife at him. He scampered off to show the other boys; free to go wherever he wanted.

My brothers and I figured out how old my mother is. In Somalia, a person's age is calculated by how many *gus* or rainy seasons they have lived. It's hard to figure exactly but we think she is fifty-seven even though she looks like eighty or ninety. I think it is because of all the pain and hardship she has endured in her life. The hard work she does every single day to stay alive shows in her body and her face. She does not have an ounce of fat anywhere and her feet are thick with calluses. They look almost like an elephant's hide, thick with cracks. Her eyes are cloudy and they don't shine in the sunshine. I am grateful that she is still able to work and that she is still really strong. Watching her work and sing I could see in her that everything works with faith. You must believe in God and all the powers that you have inside you. That is really all either one of my parents have, faith in the magic power of nature. They have no social security, no health insurance and no pension plan. My father is almost blind and my mother might weigh all of eighty pounds, but they are stronger than I am. Half of her children passed into God's hands and she carries a bullet in her chest, yet despite all the obstacles my mother has faced in her life, she is full of courage and hope.

That afternoon my father called and wondered who was around.

'It's just me, *Aba*,' I answered, walking over to where he was resting.

'Where is Mohammed?' he asked. 'It's time for my eye drops.'

'I don't know, there isn't anybody else here right now.'

'I need Mohammed or Burhaan or your mother to put the drops in my eyes,' he insisted.

He remembered me as a little girl and I had to reassure him that I could do it as well as Mama. 'Father, I am almost as tall as the boys now,' I said. 'I know what I am doing.' I gently took the bandage off and washed his face with clean water. Some of the swelling had gone down and he could chew and talk a little easier, but the eye looked frightful. The socket was shrunken and a nasty shade of yellow. When I put the drops in his eyes my father said that he could see better. 'What can you see?' I asked him.

'Shadows. I think I can see some colors and things,' he said.

'All I can say is that is really a gift from Allah,' I told him. 'I thank the Lord Allah that you even survived that encounter with the bush doctor. I hope you will go to the hospital in Galkayo from now on. Father, you don't have to go to some madman with a knife.'

'*Hiiyea*,' he said quietly and I put the bandage back on to keep the dust and flies away. I mashed up two Tylenol in his tea because he couldn't swallow them whole but he didn't drink much of the tea. At least there was one thing I brought that was useful for my family.

After we ate I told him, 'Father, I am going to come back and when I do I will stay longer,' I promised him. 'These eight days have gone by so fast. It would be much better if I could be here for two months or more and another time I will do that.'

Mohammed nodded and Rashid teased, 'Maybe you could learn to build a fire without smoking everybody out.'

'I wasn't talking to you – you bunch of useless men.' I took my father's hand and told him that I wanted my son to know his family and his people. 'When I bring Aleeke with me I'll stay for a few months. There are so many things I wanted to see; so many people I didn't even get to greet because I had so little time.'

Rashid looked puzzled and asked, 'Waris, how long have you been away?'

'Over twenty years.'

'How long did you come for?'

'A week.' My brother looked at me like I was crazy; to him it was unreal for a person to travel so far and stay for such a short time.

'That you came, Waris, that is what matters,' my father said.

My last night with my family was very special for all of us; it was a magic evening. When it got dark we spread woven mats and cloths on the ground around the fire. It was a clear night and the mosquitoes weren't bad so we all sat outside. Mother's goats wandered over and lay down near my mother. The oldest one, Whitey, snored when she fell asleep and everyone laughed at the old goat except Mama.

'Don't make fun of her,' she insisted. 'Her milk will be sour in the morning.'

'She farts a lot too,' Rashid said and my mother hissed.

I told my father, my mother, and my brothers how glad I was to have all of us together in one spot. It was a miracle for my nomadic family to be sitting together in front of a little hut. My brothers and sisters and I haven't been together in one place our whole lives.

'When is the last time when we have been gathered all together in one place?' I asked my father and mother.

My father said, 'Not ever.'

'So this is truly a great evening tonight and I thank Allah for that,' I said. Mohammed was very quiet and he turned his face up towards the zillions of stars. He's thinking about leaving tomorrow, I thought. He is thinking that we may never ever be all together again.

My mother watched her oldest son sitting quietly. 'Once there was a rich and famous sultan,' she said.

'*Hiiyea*,' her children all said together. A story! Mother's eyes shone in the firelight and she punctuated each sentence with arms and fingers across the flickering light of the fire.

'He had embroidered shirts and soft carpets. He owned a palace in Mogadishu on the shores of the Indian Ocean to catch the cool breeze. It was filled with precious jewels and silks from Arabia. The most expensive incense burned in the rooms whether he was there or not. Despite all his great wealth he was not happy and he could not understand what was wrong. He had many wives who bickered constantly, sons who fought with each other and daughters who sulked. He could buy anything he could think of but he never felt happiness or contentment. One morning after a sleepless night, he called to his servants and told them, 'Go and search until you find a truly happy man. When you find such a person bring him to me, I want to talk to him.'

The servants scoured the land and one day they noticed a poor man singing as he pulled water from a tiny well for his one skinny camel. He hummed as he milked the beast and shared the tiny bit of milk with the sultan's servants. Even with an empty stomach he laughed and joked.

'Are you a happy man?' the servants asked.

'What is there to be unhappy about?' the man answered.

'Please sir, come with me to the sultan's palace,' the oldest servant said. 'My master would like to meet you.' The poor man agreed and journeyed from the Haud into the great city of Mogadishu. He had never seen anything like it. There were so many people, so many colors, so many things to smell and taste. The sultan entertained him richly with wonderful fruits and sweetmeats, gave a lavish banquet and presented him with an embroidered *goa*.

'What is the secret of happiness?' the sultan asked perched on soft pillows. The poor man didn't know what to say, his tongue tangled with his teeth and he couldn't talk. He didn't know what made him happy when he lived in the desert – it was just the way he felt. Disappointed the sultan sent him away and the man returned to his camel and his milk bowl carved out of wood. He never forgot all the wonders of the sultan's palace and he was never happy again.'

'*Hiiyea,*' I said, because I know that story is true. Mohammed turned his face away from the firelight and wrapped his *goa* over his head.

It seemed as though the stars had babies every night,

there were so many of them. There was no sound anywhere, lovely deep silence filled up my ears. Anywhere I have been in the West you can hear the noise of a car running along a road somewhere. It never gets totally silent like the desert where there is space between the sounds. After the stories and jokes quieted down, Mama and Nhur and I went inside to sleep with the children. We could hear hyenas howling like wicked women outside the village but they don't come and bother people.

My dreams were terrible and I didn't sleep that night. I dreamed I was walking with my mother. We had been lost for a couple of days and were near death from hunger and thirst. After climbing up a big hill I saw a house with a fire and a teapot down below so I ran back to tell my mother. 'Mama, Mama, I see a house, I see people. Come, come! We are going to be OK.' I ran down the hill to the house and as I got closer I shouted, 'Hello, hello, anybody there?' No one answered, no one came out of the little hut. I could see something strange boiling up out of the spout and I looked in the teapot to see what was cooking. When we don't have much water you can cook in a teapot to conserve the water. When I took the lid off the pot it was filled with boiling blood and somebody being cooked. I dropped the lid in horror and stepped back and looked around. On each side of my shoulders there were strange people – they didn't look like normal people – they looked like white devils with sunken cheeks and hollow cloudy eyes. There were two of them on each side of me. My mother was coming down the hill behind me and I cried, 'Mama, Mama get out of here. Don't come down here – run, run away.'

She looked at me and said, 'No, Waris, you run. I can't run fast anymore. You run.' I didn't want to leave her but the evil *djinn* were coming too close. I pleaded with her,

'Mama! You gotta run with me.' She was not running fast enough and I was running, running, running. I called to her, 'Mama, slap the devils, slap them out of here!'

She shouted, 'Run, run away, Waris.'

'No, Mama,' I cried, 'what about you?'

'You run away, Waris,' she called, 'I'll be all right.' I looked back and saw that the devils were slashing at her back with long butchering knives. She fell down but when I tried to go back to her another one was after me so I had to run and couldn't help her. I was falling and screaming and I woke up screaming.

We had to leave early in the morning to get to Bosasso in one day but I could hardly get moving because I was so unhappy. My mother got up before the moon had faded away and brought her prayer mat out of her tiny hut. She unrolled it on the ground and turned her face to the holy city of Mecca, the navel of the world. She began to pray, bowing and kneeling. 'There is no God but Allah, and Mohammed is His Prophet,' she chanted. Oh, how I love the echo of that song! For my mother it is the song of life. It is her appointment calendar. She would never miss her prayers because it is a busy day. She says, I belong to Allah, that's the most important thing in my life; it is the only thing of importance. She touches eternity five times each day.

Me, I got clocks all over the house, I have watches, calendars, and date-books like the time itself is the most important thing. It's 2:00 so I'm supposed to call my booker about a job. So what if the baby is crying or the doorbell rings – somehow the little clock hands rule everything! I'm a slave to that dictator – I go out in the cold soaking rain because the little arrows must be obeyed. My mother is a slave to God. She gets dignity and strength from her God; I'm getting stressed and cold and wet.

Several doves flew down from the east and settled on the top of her little house. We call them angel birds because they wear the *tuspah*, a black necklace of feathers like a holy amulet. They bring angels and good news and I thought Allah will take care of Mother.

My dear sister-in-law Nhur made *angella* for me. When the coals of the fire burned hot and low she crouched next to it and spread the batter she beat the night before into pancakes. I couldn't take the *angella* home with me but I wanted some pictures to remind me of that special taste and smell. When I tried to photograph Nhur she picked up the long knife and poked it at me with a big smile, sticking out her tongue and jabbing at the air. 'Leave me alone, I'm cooking here,' she said.

'I know you'll use that if I get too close,' I said, but what could she do? Nhur was very pregnant and wearing a long dress. I filmed her from every angle just to tease her. She wasn't going to run after me and let the *angella* burn.

The neighbors came over to see what they could get. They knew I was leaving and would not need to carry things back with me. 'Give me the cocoa butter; give me that scarf!' they cried. 'You don't need that anymore.' I didn't have much to give, but I gave them whatever I could. It's a Somali garage sale.

There are times when the sun races across the sky and that morning was one of them. That's another problem with clocks; time isn't always the same. My father was resting inside Burhaan's house and I went to say goodbye to him first. My body was heavy and hard to move; I felt like I weighed ten tons. There is a Somali word that means talking to a person for the last time before a journey. I started crying as soon as *Aba* said it. He was so helpless and weak. He heard me and asked, 'What are you crying about, child?'

'I wish you could see my face before I leave.'

'Baby, you know that I can't see you.'

A bandage covered one eye, the other was cloudy, and both were sightless. 'I want you to see me – my face, my eyes; to take a good look at me,' I told him. 'It has been more than twenty years since you last saw me. Do you remember what I look like? I am a grown woman now – I was a little girl when I left.' He reached up and I took his hand and placed it on my face so he could feel my skin, the shape of my nose. His touch was shy and tender. More tears welled up in my eyes and wet his fingers. I wanted to see the cocky strong father that I used to know. I longed for the powerful father who frightened me more than lions.

My father read my thoughts and said, 'Waris, we all age and change and nothing can ever be the same.'

'I guess there is a reason for everything but only Allah knows the reason for this,' I sobbed. Everybody was waiting for me and I heard Mohammed calling and beeping the horn outside. 'Daddy, I've got to go now,' I said.

My father said, 'I have something for my grandson; a *xudden-xir*,' and he handed me a long hair plucked from a female camel. It is a gift for a newborn child. It made me cry even harder. 'Do me a favor,' he whispered, 'don't let them see you cry, you are a grown woman. I'm not dead – cry when I'm dead. Now get out of here.' That was his way of saying I love you. He wanted to make me tough because that is what he knows about life and getting through it.

'You know, Papa,' I said, 'remember the other day when everybody was sitting around talking and somebody said, "Waris, you look like your father," and other people said, "No, you look like your mother, you're the spitting image of your mother." Papa, I know what I am. I got hardheaded strength from my father's side and wisdom and looks from my mother. Everybody laughed then – but you know that it's true.'

He said, 'Remember that, Waris – you got my strength – keep that strength, keep it always.'

I had learned what gift my family needed and I knew that they would never ask for it. '*Aba*, I will send the money for Nhur's bride price as soon as I get to a bank,' I told him. He took my hand and held it next to his heart. My father turned to the wall and I know he cried when I left – but he would not let me see it.

As soon as I came out crying – my mother said, 'Hey, wait a minute! How come I never get the crying? Why are you crying for him and not for me?'

'Mama, please come back with me!' I took her hands and pleaded with her.

'Waris, I can't come with you now,' she said. 'I've got your father and Mohammed *Inyer*.'

'Mama, I'll come back and get you and bring you to New York with me.'

She said, 'Waris, I'm too old for those countries. I hated Abu Dhabi when I was there with your sister. I saw the piles of gold jewelry and a big tree made of gold. You look in the streets and there are little children gnawing on a bone and starving to death, sick and nobody cares. I can't live there.'

'Mama, New York is not like that.'

'Who am I going to talk to? I don't speak anything but Somali. Who am I going to go visit? All my friends are here.' She took my hands and walked with me to the waiting car while she talked. 'Baby,' she said, 'I didn't like Abu Dhabi and over there is the most like here. It is hot like Africa – people pray five times a day, but they don't mean it. How can they walk right past those hungry children?'

I said, 'Mama please, I need you.'

She shook her head, 'I don't need over there. This is my home and this is what I know and this is where I'm going to die.' She was right. I could not imagine her being in New York City. My Mama, she wouldn't last a day, she would be miserable. She would miss her way of knowing. I knew she wouldn't be able to get up in the morning and just go – she would have nowhere to go. Nobody in New York would understand a joke about a goat farting. Who would she joke with? She winked at me. 'I can't leave my children – I have to stay here in case the biggest one, your father, can't find himself another wife.'

'Mama,' I said, 'you need somebody to take care of you for a change. Please come with me.' I desperately wanted to bring her home with me – but it was a selfish wish. I wanted to bring her peace to my house in New York – to my son, to my life.

She drew me close to her, kissed my forehead, and said, 'No. I am here where God put me.' My mother is the unmovable foundation of our family; she is the tree with roots all the way down to heaven.

'Oh, Mama!' I cried and hugged her for the last time. I hugged Burhaan and Rashid, Ragge, Uncle Ahmed, little Asha, and Nhur. Rashid smiled and pointed to his beautiful row of perfect white teeth. Then he handed me about ten *caday* tooth sticks he cut fresh that morning. I laughed and put them in my bag to take back to New York. Mohammed and I got into the car and I watched everybody that I love get smaller and smaller as we drove over the little hills and on to Borama road back towards Bosasso. I was sobbing and I couldn't stop. My Mama! I love that woman. She has a grace and a dignity I'm never going to have. She was born a Somali woman and she is going to stay a Somali woman. She accepts where Allah placed her on the earth and she is thanking him every day for that. She doesn't want to question God; she's already safe with him. Me – I couldn't accept it, I had to run off and get all confused. I wish I had that part of her, that acceptance, but I don't. I felt, deep in my bones, that this life was not right for me, so I ran off. Honestly it didn't shock me or sadden me when my mother refused to come back with me. I understood exactly what she was saying. It's not hard to be in a Somali village if you were born there and raised there and you don't know anything else. She has something that is greater than all the wealth in the West. She has acceptance and peace in her life.

14

journey back

Women are the devil's snares

Somali Proverb

The journey back to the little airport at Bosasso was completely different than the trip to my mother's village. This
time the dirt track was full of thick red mud and potholes of
brown water. In some places the road was more like a river.
You have to keep the car moving in mud so again we
bounced all over the place and you had to hang on or else
you might hit your head or fall over. If you get stuck there is
nothing to do but wait until another car or truck comes
along to help you get out. However, everywhere I looked it
was lush green and beautiful. The sky had big puffy clouds
hanging there and the temperature was comfortable. I sat in
the back seat and cried because it was so hard to leave my
parents. I prayed to Allah that my father would be all right,
that I would see him again. Mohammed and the driver we

hired, Musa, talked about how hot it had been the day we arrived. Musa said that some people had been out in the sun and had died from the terrible heat.

We traveled hard all that day in order to get back to Bosasso by dark. Musa was Daarood, and a friend of Mohammed's. He didn't stop for hours. He had never been to Bosasso and I wondered how he knew where he was going with no maps and no signs. Often tracks went off into different directions and none of them seemed bigger than the others. *Djinn* hang out at the intersections of roads and I hoped one would not jump in the car and play tricks on us. Musa never hesitated though – he just kept driving on and on away from the sun in the morning and towards the sunset in the afternoon. *Dikdik* darted through the scrub – they look like tiny deer on spindly legs. We passed a long-necked gerenuk, a kind of antelope, on its hind legs, stripping an acacia bush. It was too intent on eating to be disturbed by a car passing by. Old man baboon and his troop barked defiance from a hilltop showing us his big teeth and long hairy arms.

Late that afternoon, I was so hungry I said, 'Hey, I can't take much more. I am starving back here and I really need to stop for a little while.'

'OK,' Musa agreed, 'I know a tea shop not too far from here. We can stop there and eat.'

'What do they have?' I thought about a big plate of something good like rice and spiced goat meat or a shish kebab. I hoped they would have camel milk. I had been looking for it the entire time I was home but there was none in my mother's village. It had been so dry that the camels were not giving milk. Camel milk is rich and so nutritious that people can live on it. I remembered the three-cornered *zambusi* that are made to break the fast during the month of

Ramadan and sweet tea with cardamom and milk. I was so hungry, I think my stomach was flat up against my backbone.

'I don't know what they will have left this late in the day, everything might be almost gone by now but they will have something and it's a good place to eat,' Musa said. 'I've eaten there before.'

He slowed down and stopped in front of a ramshackle restaurant set a little way back from the edge of the road. It wasn't much of a village; there was a gas station, the tea shop and a few huts in the back. The restaurant was basically a large open area covered with a red tin roof. The kitchen area was behind it and smoke from the fire drifted straight up because there wasn't any wind. The terrace had been built in the shade of some big trees so that a breeze would come in. I was surprised to see at least fifty to sixty men just sitting there at broken down old metal tables and wooden benches. It was such a tiny village I didn't know where they all came from, or why these men were just sitting around.

Musa and Mohammed with his long legs walked in front of me and through the restaurant. As soon as I set foot in the place I heard men muttering, 'Oh no! Oh no, no,' then, 'what is she doing?' I ignored them and kept right on walking inside. As I tried to pass through the tables to the kitchen in the back, a man came over and stepped right in front of me. He apparently was the waiter but he didn't have an apron on or look especially clean. He blocked my path when I tried to go around him and said, 'Excuse me, excuse me.' I ignored him and he must have decided that I didn't speak Somali. He started shouting and waving his hands in my face. 'Hey! Hey! Hey!' he bellowed but I just kept walking towards my brother. I didn't feel like explaining myself to a man with sweaty armpits and dirty fingernails.

Suddenly several men started shouting at him, 'Stop her! Get her out of here.' The waiter came and directly blocked my path.

I looked at him right in the eyes and said, 'Is there a problem? *Warrier, Maa'hah d'ih?*' – I said it in Somali so he knew that I understood everything that had been said.

He refused to look in my face but hissed at me like I was a stray chicken he wanted to shoo back out the door, 'You can't come in here,' he said loudly. 'This is just for men, the women go elsewhere.'

'What? What are you talking about? Why can't I eat here if I want to?' I asked. Although Somali women won't eat in restaurants with men it was news to me that women weren't allowed to eat with men when they wanted to.

He repeated, 'This restaurant is for men only, no women are allowed in here.'

'That's ridiculous. I am not going to bother anybody.'

'I told you to get out,' he said spitting the words at me and puffing himself up with self-importance. I was so shocked that I didn't know what to do. Mohammed was only thinking about food and Musa was in a hurry to get back on the road. The nasty man would not even let me pass to tell them what was going on – he stood his ground between me and the kitchen. I was furious, but I was starving because we hadn't eaten all day. Standing as tall as I could I snarled at the skinny little man, 'Well, where do the women go?'

He said, 'Over there, back over there,' and pointed his long bony finger back out the door as if somehow I had violated the filthy dump with a dirt floor and beat-up tables held together with wire.

Meanwhile Mohammed looked back to see what happened to me. He needed money from me to pay for the food he had ordered and must have wondered where I was.

He came over and asked the greasy waiter, 'What's the problem?'

The waiter suddenly became polite and told him, 'I'm sorry, but no women are allowed in here. The women go back over there, they eat in another room.'

My brother looked up and down at this man with narrow eyes and a filthy shirt. He noticed that the place was quiet and every single man there was waiting to see what would happen. He shook his head at me and asked him, 'Well, where is the other room? Show us the room for women.'

The waiter led us outside, everything was quiet except for his cheap Chinese flip-flops slapping on the dirt. We walked all the way around the terrace and the trees to a little area set apart from the rest of the restaurant. He pointed to a tattered hut that was literally in the back of the bathroom, turned on his rubber heel, and slapped back into the restaurant.

The bathroom was not a nice room with tiled walls and a white porcelain toilet to sit on and flush, I didn't expect that. It was a Somali long drop; a deep hole dug into the ground. It was dirty and full of flies and big toast-colored cockroaches. They are fearless and will crawl right out of that stinky hole while you are hanging over it or into your food. It smelled so my eyes stung and flies came out of the dark corners and swarmed all over us. One wall of the bathroom was part of the women's eating room. It was nothing but three ramshackle walls and a dusty floor. There wasn't even a table or chairs in the place, just an old bench with a broken leg. I thought I was going to cry. My mother wouldn't keep her goats in such a terrible place. All the men were sitting like kings enjoying the shade in the restaurant while women were supposed to eat in a place full of shit.

I looked at my brother and he looked at me. Even though

he was acting like a big Somali man this was too much for him too. He shook his head and said, 'Fuck this.' We turned around and walked back around to the car. Mohammed said, 'Well what do you want to do?'

'Are there any other places we can get something to eat around here?' I asked Musa. 'I am starving.'

Mohammed agreed, 'I'm hungry too.'

Musa shook his head, 'Sorry, but there are no other places to eat anywhere near by.'

'Waris, did you say something to the waiter?' Mohammed asked like I had somehow insulted him.

'A woman walking into the place was an insult to that baboon,' I said.

'Let's try and talk to the cook. He seemed like a reasonable enough person,' Mohammed said and he went around the back to the kitchen area to talk to the cook. 'Excuse me, but I won't put my sister in that place – it's filthy back there,' he told him. 'All we want to do, we are just passing through, is to eat something and we will continue on our way.'

The cook listened to what he had to say but he was just as insistent as the waiter. 'I'm sorry but no women are allowed.'

My brother said, 'What exactly do you mean when you say no women allowed? We are hungry. Do you have some food?'

The cook said, 'Yes.'

'Are you selling it?'

'Yes.'

'Serving it?'

'Yes.'

'Well,' Mohammed said calmly, 'she is a human being isn't she? What is the big problem? All we want to do is have something to eat.' The cook just stood there and Mohammed decided not to push it any further. He said,

'OK, I understand that women cannot eat in here. Can you let my sister just sit outside for a minute and we will take some food with us.'

But the cook said, 'No.' He shook his head and became very surly. 'I told you that no women are allowed in here. Ever.' He stood there in a ragged shirt and worn out *maa-a-weiss* and crossed his arms over his chest like he was some royal lord or something.

My brother stood his ground and then he said, 'You know what? Fuck you and your food, *Aba'ha Wuss*.' He looked at me and he said, 'Come on Waris, let's get out of here.' I said not a word and I proudly followed my brother out of that place.

We got back in the car and drove off, kicking up a cloud of dust. Musa looked over at Mohammed and said, 'The food in there is rubbish anyway.'

I was so pleased at my brother actually taking my part that I wanted to hug him and cheer. He was fuming at the whole thing. 'This country is going nowhere if these people can't change some of the old, stupid traditions. It's crazy!'

I was glad my brother had started to see things differently. 'That is the ignorant bush mentality that is keeping this country down,' I said. 'Women and men don't eat together. A woman can't cut a man's hair, women are sewn shut. Women are not looked at as equal to men in any aspect of life.' I told Mohammed, 'I respect that people feel that way, I don't try to change the way they see things, but all the same I don't understand why they need to push their views down my throat.'

'It's got to change, Waris,' he said. 'When you treat women like dirt, it's easy to treat people from other tribes just as badly. It's got to change.'

Mohammed, you are one who has changed, I thought to myself, and tears of pride ran down my cheeks.

15

desert dawn

So give to the kinsman his due,
And to the needy, and to the wayfarer.
That is best for those
Who seek Allah's countenance.

Koran, Sura 30: 38–9,
The Romans

Musa crawled furiously across the belly of Somalia, from the Ethiopian border to the Indian Ocean. We passed the villages of Garowe, Nugal and Qardho. They were larger than my mother's settlement but still had no electricity, latrines, schools, or hospitals. There were puddles as big as lakes and ruts in the road up to my knees. We slipped and skidded over and into some pretty deep mud holes but Musa always managed to get the tires to catch on to something. We slid out the other side and on to dry ground more times than I care to remember.

Late in the afternoon we stopped by a river to wash our faces and cool off. Water in the desert is always rushing somewhere else. Starlings, with brilliant coats of blue and gold, flashed in the sun as they flew away. Two peacocks calmly waddled away. They are good luck – especially if you see two of them, however it's bad luck if you only see feathers. Mohammed took off his shoes and waded in the water. 'If only we had rivers like this all over the country Somalia would certainly be the most beautiful place on earth,' I said. Like a thirsty lion I wanted to stick my mouth in the clear water. I washed my face and arms but I wanted to take my clothes off and go for a swim. I hiked up my dress but Mohammed kept telling me to put my dress down. A camel with its front legs tied together hopped slowly down to the river for a drink. The hobble keeps it from wandering too far. 'That's how I feel about these dresses and headscarves,' I told Mohammed. 'You can't move because they trip you.'

'When are you going to stop running around anyway?' he asked.

I gave up on Mohammed ever really understanding my point of view and went back to dipping my scarf in the water and washing my face with it. Musa noticed a land tortoise next to the road. It looked at us with tiny black eyes but pulled into its shell as soon as I went over for a closer look. 'Maybe it's a spirit guide come to tell me something,' I said. 'This tortoise means my home is safe.'

By the time I could catch the smell of the Indian Ocean and see the lights of Bosasso it was long after the town had gone to bed. It was so quiet I could hear the waves lapping at the shore on the edge of town. Musa took us to a hotel and Mohammed went inside to get rooms and see if he could find anything to eat. I wanted a cool shower and a bed almost more than food. I really didn't think anything would be still open. People eat their main meal in the middle of the day and restaurants are not open after dark because the electricity is not very reliable. Mohammed tried several hotels but they didn't have any rooms. Musa took us down a side street to another hotel. It was not very nice, but I didn't really care, I was so tired. I went inside with Mohammed.

'No, nothing tonight,' the short attendant in the lobby informed us. He stood up and rubbed his eyes. His beard was dyed red from henna and his face was framed with the white hair on his head.

'Why don't you have any rooms?' Mohammed asked. 'The other hotels were full too.'

'Lots of people are waiting for the plane to Abu Dhabi,' he said, pointing to all the people hanging out in the lobby. 'There are people here working on many different projects for the United Nations and many other agencies. The place is full of construction these days! Everybody is coming and going all the time, except for last week.' Three of his bottom teeth were missing and the rest were black from chewing *khat*. 'The plane didn't land because there were some goats on the runway. Oh, that pilot was so mad, he turned around and went back to Abu Dhabi!' he said laughing.

I didn't think it was funny. I needed to get back to New York and I certainly didn't want to hang around Bosasso for a week because they couldn't keep animals off the runway. We didn't have boarding passes or confirmed seats – you go to the airport and wait in line. I looked at Mohammed and said, 'I hope we get on the flight! Do you think it will be a problem?'

'I'll go to the airport now and find out how to get on the plane.' He turned back to the clerk and asked, 'Is there another hotel in town?'

'I don't think you will find anything available tonight – it's late and there are only a few hotels in Bosasso. This town is so busy everything is full all the time.'

As we stood there trying to think of what to do a man I didn't know came up and asked Mohammed, 'Are you Mohammed Dirie?'

'My father is Dahee Dirie,' Mohammed replied. They talked about my father, but I was so tired I couldn't really think straight. The man had a round belly and wore the embroidered hat that means he has made the *Hajj* to Mecca. 'Waris, this is Hajji Suliman,' Mohammed told me. 'He is related on both the Majeerteen and Hawiye side of our family.'

Hajji glanced at me and told Mohammed, 'Your sister can have my hotel room tonight.'

I couldn't believe his generosity. He offered his bed to a stranger just because we are from the same family. For a moment I couldn't think what to say. In the West when such a gift is offered you must say, 'Oh no, I couldn't put you out.' You refuse the offer and if the person still insists, you can accept. However, that's the way a guest is treated in my country, it was the way everyone had been most of the trip. If I refused, Hajji would be insulted. 'Thank you, thank you,' I told him.

Mohammed and I followed Hajji to his room. He took his belongings and gave me the key. He warned me to lock myself in and to lock the door whenever I went out. 'Where are you going to sleep?' I asked Mohammed.

'I'll sleep outside, don't worry about it,' he said and left to see what he could find out at the airport.

My heart sank when I went into the room, and I didn't know what to do. It was unbearable. Even though it was over 100 degrees I had to close the door and lock it. When I opened the little window there was no breeze at all. Nothing was moving. Worst of all it was filthy and stank of sweat and urine. I wanted a cool shower and clean sheets. Hajji

Suliman's tiny room had a concrete floor and a cot thing – there was no bathroom. There was a ceiling fan but it didn't work. Mohammed would put his *goa* on the ground and settle down to sleep in the fresh clean air, washed by the sea.

The bed was a sort of a battered mat stretched over a wooden frame with no comfort to it at all. What could I say? I didn't complain – because I don't want to be an ungrateful bitch – but it was full of holes and it stank. I would rather have slept outside with the men, but I couldn't.

For the first time I was thankful for a long dress; I tucked it around my legs and pulled my scarf over my head to keep bugs out. Sleep would not come because of the heat and I was afraid of rats. In the darkness I heard something scratching around and spent most of the night trying to see what was making noise and praying that I didn't see a rat.

Even before the first glimmer of light I heard the call to prayers. It must have been around four in the morning. The muezzin climbs to the top of the minaret in the mosque and chants, 'There is no God but God and Mohammed is his Prophet.' When they pray it echoes in every direction. It was amazing to hear the prayer drift through the entire town. Every prayer, five times a day is the same thing. Everything stops and everything echoes with prayer. It is the only clock worth paying attention to.

Mohammed came to get me in the morning and we had tea and waited for Musa but he never showed up. Mohammed decided that he had collapsed from exhaustion. The man drove constantly to make a living. Mohammed had not been able to talk to anyone the night before and so we hired another car to take us out to the airport to make sure that we could get on the next flight. Several men wanted to go to the airport and two more waved and asked for a ride as we rode out of town. The car was packed, but we were happy to be able to help. The early morning is the hottest time of the day because there is no breeze off the water. The blue sea shimmering in the distance caught my eye as we approached the airport. 'Which road takes you to the ocean?' I asked, longing for a cool swim.

'What does she want to know that for?' a tall man with a long tribal scar on his cheek asked Mohammed.

'Hello,' I said. 'You don't need to talk to my brother. I am sitting right here.'

'What is she going to do in the ocean?' he continued to ignore me and talked to Mohammed.

'Look at my clothes, they are dripping I am so hot,' I said. 'I intend to cool off in the water and have a swim.'

'You better tell her that we don't swim here,' he announced to Mohammed. 'We are desert people.'

When we got to the airport Mohammed went into the brick building and I waited for him in the car. He returned with bad news. Damal Airlines would not arrive for two days and we would just have to sit in Bosasso.

'What!' I cried. 'First it took us a day to come to Bosasso from Galkayo. Then it will be two more days before the flight! Mohammed, I could have stayed with Mama another day. Why did we have to come back here so early? We didn't need to get here until tomorrow!'

'You have to stay in Bosasso to make sure you get on the flight because this is the only airplane,' Mohammed said. 'They don't have boarding passes – you just have to be there to make sure you get on the plane.'

'That is a ridiculous way to run an airline,' I said. 'We are wasting two days – two days I could have been with my family.'

'Well, that's the way things are around here. Don't worry – we will get on the plane when it comes.'

'*Enshallah*, if Allah wills,' I said, finding my mother's words on my lips. Allah has a plan for you, she told me and I decided to use the time to talk to people about United Nations projects. I wanted to see first-hand what their needs were – to find out the best ways to help.

Mohammed introduced me to another relative, another man who knew our father. Abdillahi Aden was the airport director and he arranged for us to get on the plane without personally waiting in line. Abdillahi came back into town with us and talked about the many projects in Bosasso.

'When people are full of hope they want to work and be a part of building something,' he said. 'The government in Somaliland has provided a degree of stability and is one that the people can respect,' he told us. 'There are a lot of people who come to live here in Bosasso. The town is growing and getting bigger every day.'

Mohammed explained, 'My sister is from New York and this is her first trip back to Somalia for over twenty years.'

'*Hiiyea*! New York! I heard that is a very dangerous place,' said Abdillahi.

'It can be,' I told him.

'I heard they eat dogs.'

'No,' I said, 'they don't eat dogs.'

'He means hot dogs,' Mohammed interrupted. 'Europeans and Americans eat something called hot dogs. But they aren't dog, it's pig.'

'What a terrible place,' Abdillahi said with grave sympathy and I finally realized he was teasing me. 'When are you two coming back to Somalia to live? It's safe here now, you should come back and stop eating dogs and pigs.' Abdillahi urged Mohammed to return and work to build the country but Mohammed looked away.

After lunch Abdillahi showed us another hotel. They had

only one room available with two narrow wooden cots but the room was clean and had a bathroom. It was humble but Mohammed and I were happy to have it. I took a shower in salt water piped in from the ocean and was grateful to God for the blessing of water.

There was a United Nations sign on a cinder block building not too far from our hotel and Mohammed and I walked over in the late afternoon. Everything closed in the hottest part of the day and opened back up after the afternoon meal and rest. Several men sat inside and the person in charge said he was from Sierra Leone. He didn't have the evenly spaced Somali features – his nose was too big and his skin was pock-marked.

'What kind of project is this?' I asked. He gave me a funny look when I started to talk. 'My name is Waris Dirie and I will be back at the United Nations in New York in a day or two. I have a big meeting there and I want to bring back some information about the projects in Bosasso. Can I ask you some questions about what is going on here?'

He pulled at his bottom lip and stared at the table without answering. Finally he turned to Mohammed and said suspiciously, 'Who do you work for? What do you want here?'

'My name is Waris Dirie and I work with the United Nations,' I repeated.

He totally ignored me like I was deaf or blind and kept asking Mohammed, 'Who are you? What do you want?'

I came over to stand right in front of him so that he would have to look at me. 'Excuse me,' I said, 'I am talking to you.'

'What are you doing here? What is this all about?' he started to scream at the top of his lungs. All the time he looked at my brother.

There were two other guys in chairs in the back of the room and one of them looked intelligent so I said to him, 'Hey, brother, could you please help me out here?'

He looked at me and at the old man who was screaming, then he turned to his friend and said, 'Let's get out of here.'

That seemed suspicious and made me more determined to find out about the project. I turned back to the man from Sierra Leone and said, 'Sir, excuse me, with all due respect, look me in the face. I am talking to you – this guy is not talking to you, he is not asking you questions – please look at me.' That angry man raised up his hand like he was going to push me but he stopped when Mohammed stood up. Mohammed did not say anything – he towered above both of us. Then my brother calmly explained that we were only gathering information – that we were not looking to report any wrongdoing.

'You have to be specific. What exactly do you want?' the man said pulling on his lip again.

'I do apologize if you felt I was spying on you. I would like to have information about women and children, especially about women's health and the United Nations projects to help them.'

'Ah,' he said, 'I cannot help you with that. There are people who talk about that kind of thing in another building – over there.' He pointed to a cement brick building around the corner.

We found the building and the sign above the door identified it as a United Nations project. About six or seven men were sitting inside the single room playing the game of *shax*. In *shax* there are two players. One man draws three squares in the dirt, one inside the other. Each player puts down twelve small stones at the intersections of the squares. If you can get three in a row you win one of your opponent's pieces. They hardly even looked up when we walked in. When the game was over they greeted us with suspicion. It was the same reaction as the first place. Everybody thought I was trying to get money from them even though I explained that I was a peaceful volunteer. 'I am not here to look for work or to interfere with you,' I told them. 'I came simply because I am concerned. I love my country and I thought I could help. I am going back to New York and I have a meeting with the big boys at the United Nations next week. I want to bring back some information. I'd like to know what you need and how we can help.' These men stood there shifting from one foot to another and choosing every word carefully no matter what I said. 'The most important thing that I can take back is information about what you need,' I repeated. 'I don't want anything from you, I am here to help.' They stood there uneasily and offered nothing. I was disgusted and confronted them. 'Why don't you help me to help you? What's the matter?' But no one would talk to me – they wouldn't trust me no matter what I said. They didn't want to talk to a woman.

When we left Mohammed told me, 'Women just can't do that, Waris. You can't go into a place and ask men questions. Women don't do that here.'

'I don't believe you people,' I told him. 'How are you going to change with this kind of attitude and way of doing things?' On the way back to the hotel I saw another low building with a UN sign. I looked in through the window and saw some women inside. They greeted me warmly and directed me to the woman who was in charge of health and education for children and women. Mohammed and I found her office in a group of low prefabricated buildings just at the edge of town. Assia Adan was a dignified woman with a direct manner. She was a great source of information.

Assia told me that her mission is to try and educate the women about health. She is a midwife and offers medical care as well as teaching about the dangers of FGM.

'We have lessons on the dangers of infection and we talk about the girls who have died.'

I remembered my beautiful sister who died after her infibulation.

'Of course we would like to eradicate this practice completely, but it is very hard to get people to even talk about it. The mothers don't even question that it is the right thing to do for their daughters. It is unimaginable for them not to have their daughters done.'

I agreed and said, 'My mother didn't think she was hurting me. She believed I would be pure and clean.'

Assia and I both knew that in my country they practice the most severe form, pharonic infibulation, where the entire inner lips of the labia and the clitoris are removed and the opening is sewn shut.

'My mother was very careful that I slept on my back after it was done, so that the wound would close smooth and flat. It was very important to her that my body was perfectly flat and smooth. What do you do to change that?' I said.

Assia explained that they were trying to teach mothers about Sunni circumcision, which involves no actual cutting and sewing, and is instead just a ritual. Apparently, some modern women in Saudi Arabia have taken this up as an alternative.

'I wasn't able to get a single person in my village to talk about this with me. Not one person! They all looked at me like I was crazy.'

'Yes,' Assia sympathized. 'We are only beginning – I have been at work here for six years and we haven't made any progress – but we are still here. That's the good news. We

have not been forced to leave or stop. Frankly, I consider
even a toe-hold here an important step. There is hope.'

I smiled. 'I can feel the hope. I was afraid to come back
to my own country for fear that someone would attack me
because I publicly speak out against FGM. People warned
me that I might be detained at the border, kidnapped or
worse. Assia, I'll be back and we are going to work
together,' I promised her. 'I am going to help you in every
way I can.' I told her about the plans for my Foundation,
Desert Dawn, and the money we are going to raise to help
women and children. We plan to build a community
health center in Bosasso, provide educational seminars for
women and fund mobile units to provide healthcare and
education for nomad families in remote areas. I gave her a
hug and a kiss. As long as there are people like Assia there
is a way.

Mohammed was so tall that I took two steps for every one
of his. It was hard to keep up with him when we walked
through town back to our hotel, especially with a long dress
dragging in the mud and wrapping around my ankles. I
scurried after him and held my dress high so I could walk
better. Two women were sitting on a stoop when I passed.
'Look at that! Her dress is up over her waist.'

'Well, she can't be Somali – walking like that.'

When we went out to eat that evening I took my camera
with me so I could get some shots of the town and the different UN projects. After we ate, I saw a beautiful poster
with wonderful colors and a map. I picked up the camera
and took a shot of it with the flash. Suddenly a big rock hit
my thigh. I jumped in pain and saw an entire cart of soda
bottles tumble over and break all over the street. The boy
who threw the rock at me must have slammed into the bottles with his arm and sent them flying. God took care of

them, I thought. I didn't wait around to see what would happen next and ran to get in the car with Mohammed.

'Someone hit me with a rock!' I cried to my brother.

He was calmly cleaning his teeth with a tooth stick and looked over at me and shook his head. Always the comic Mohammed replied, 'They should have shot you too.'

'You bastard! I could have been hurt.'

'Waris, I have told you again and again, don't take pictures – they will kill you. You know that some people here truly believe that a picture will take your spirit. That is the way they feel, little sister. To you it's nothing but here it is disrespectful. I'd do the same if some strange woman stuck a camera in my face.'

That night several ladies sat in the hotel lobby sipping tea. We started to talk and an elegant lady said they were Somali too. She said, 'You know, you look like this lady I saw on TV.'

I wondered where she had a television and asked, 'Where are you from?'

'Sweden. I live in Sweden.'

'You saw a Somali woman on Swedish television?'

'Yes! But I can't remember her name. She is on TV in Germany.'

'Oh,' I said. 'What does this woman do?'

'She speaks out against female circumcision.'

'Well what do you think about that?' I asked her quietly.

'I think it's about time somebody spoke out about it! I am so proud of this Somali woman,' she said with flashing eyes. 'We definitely don't talk about that! She is so brave, I love her. She gives us all courage and hope that things will change.'

I asked, 'Do you know her name?'

'I think it's Waris,' she said. 'Are you sure you're not her?'

'No, I'm not very brave,' I replied, my head down.

How foolish I had been. I was ashamed. Why had I been so scared to come back to Somalia? Why did I think that they were going to kill me? My own people knew about me and they still loved me! When everybody in New York said, 'Don't go. Don't go to Somalia, it's too dangerous,' I hardly questioned them. I never thought, hey, I know my people, why would they harm me? When the news reported that Somalia was a war zone I didn't question it. When I got to Somalia I was just like anyone, anywhere. Not for one minute did I feel any fear. I felt angry at the way some men treated me because I am a woman, but from most people all I heard was welcome, welcome. 'Do you want me to show you this? Let me show you around. Have you been here? Have you seen this? You can't go back without seeing this,' people said. Maybe there is a crazy clan somewhere, but khat-crazed soldiers with guns never threatened me. I saw a beautiful country and my beautiful people.

It's easy to stand up and speak out about something far away – it's easy to talk about FGM to a room of strangers. It takes courage to risk disapproval among your own family, to question the beliefs of someone who stands in front of you. Talking about FGM in the West was easy – the real battle is in Somalia. Allah led me back to my country so that I would know what has to be done. I pray that he will give me the strength to speak to my own people in a way that they can hear and understand. My visit showed me how difficult it will be for people to change – but I am filled with hope. I love my country. If you ask me right this minute where I want to be – I'll sing about Africa. 'Hello Africa! How are you doing? I'm feeling good and I hope you are too.'

Desert Dawn, Waris Dirie's foundation, is a non-profit organisation with a simple and yet profound mission to empower the children of Somalia with better health, education and opportunity.

Desert Dawn will work at grassroots level to assist others who share Waris' vision of a new Somalia where famine, disease and violence no longer threaten to destroy the lives, hopes and dreams of childhood.

Desert Dawn Inc
320 East 65th Street
Suite 116
New York
NY 10021

www.desertdawn.org

Join the Fight Against FGM

If you would like to help us fight the mutilation of millions of girls, you can send contributions to a special trust that has been set aside to eliminate female genital mutilation. These funds will be used to promote educational and outreach programs in twenty-three countries. To learn more about this program write to:

The Campaign to Eliminate FGM
UNFPA (United Nations Population Fund)
605 Third Avenue
New York, NY 10158
USA

World Wide Web: http://www.unfpa.org